Irus Braverman's newest  eloquent and lucid style proximity, anatomically and ethically, to our animal brethren, including those with fins and gills.

— Richard M. Ratzan, editor of
Imagining Vesalius

Braverman's innovative ethnographic foray into the work of zoo and aquaria veterinarians could not be more timely. *Zoo Veterinarians* incisively underscores the need for global health frameworks to adopt a multispecies orientation that brings medicine into closer conversation with the social sciences to understand diseases and their possible cures. Immensely readable and thought-provoking, *Zoo Veterinarians* will appeal to scholars and lay readers alike.

— Maneesha Deckha, University of Victoria

Animal welfare—or conservation? Irus Braverman takes us behind the scenes in zoos and aquariums to witness the daily work of the ultimate general practitioner: the veterinarian who may daily need to treat a dozen different species. In an era of ecological crisis, she passionately argues the importance of interdisciplinary meddling and open conversation between experts and outsiders.

— John Law, author of *After Method: Mess in Social Science Research*

In this vividly written and deeply empathetic book, Braverman takes us on a journey into the world of zoo and aquarium veterinarians as they grapple with the scientific and ethical challenges of caring for wild animals in an increasingly human-made world. Inspiring and troubling in equal measure, *Zoo Veterinarians* shows us how necessary and how hard it is to balance the wellbeing of individuals, species, and ecosystems, to engage responsibly with the fleshy materiality of diverse animals, and to build bridges between veterinary experts and all the rest of us who care deeply about the fate of wild animals.

— Etienne Benson, author of
Wired Wilderness

In this original and uniquely perceptive book, Braverman delicately documents and examines the work of zoo and aquarium veterinarians, whether it concerns a supernumerary giraffe or a cross river puffer fish with skin problems. In doing so, she provides a wonderfully insightful account not only of veterinarians and animals but also of the practices, materials, bodies and concerns that bind them together.

— Henry Buller, coauthor of
Food and Animal Welfare

Zoo veterinarians are a critical but poorly documented community at the heart of the modern zoo. With this engaging behind-the-scenes study, Braverman brings their work into the light, showing how these versatile professionals are also playing an increasingly important role in advancing wildlife and ecological health outside zoo walls. This book should be read by everyone who cares about zoos, animals, and the concerns and responsibilities shaping our shared welfare on the planet.

— Ben A. Minteer, author of
The Fall of the Wild

Zoo Veterinarians

Governing Care on a Diseased Planet

Despite their centrality to the operation of contemporary accredited zoo and aquarium institutions, the work of zoo veterinarians has rarely, if ever, been the focus of a critical analysis in the social science and humanities. Drawing on in-depth interviews and observations of zoo and aquarium veterinarians in Europe and North America, this book highlights the recent transformation that has occurred in the zoo veterinarian profession, and what this transformation can teach us about our rapidly changing planet. In an age of mass extinction, climate change, and emerging zoonotic diseases, the role of zoo veterinarians is shifting from caring for individual animals to caring for diverse species, resilient ecosystems, and planetary health.

Zoo veterinarians, in other words, are "going wild." Originally an individual welfare-centered profession, these experts are increasingly concerned with the sustainability of wild animal populations and with ecological health. In this sense, the story of zoo vets "going wild"—in their subjects of care, their motivations, and their ethical standards, as well as in their professional practices and scientific techniques—is also a story about zoo animals gone wild, wild animals encroaching on the zoo, and, more generally, a wild world that is becoming "zoo-ified." Such transformations have challenged existing norms of veterinary practice. Exploring the regulatory landscape that governs the work of zoo and aquarium veterinarians, Braverman traverses the gap between the hard and soft sciences and between humans and nonhumans.

At the intersection of animal studies, socio-legal studies, and Science and Technology Studies, this book will appeal not only to those interested in zoos and in animal welfare, but also to scholars in the posthumanities.

Irus Braverman is Professor of Law and Adjunct Professor in Geography at the University at Buffalo, the State University of New York. She has authored and edited nine books, including *Zooland: The Institution of Captivity* (2012), *Wild Life: The Institution of Nature* (2015), and *Coral Whisperers: Scientists on the Brink* (2018).

Law, Science and Society
Series editors:
John Paterson, University of Aberdeen, UK
Julian Webb, University of Melbourne, Australia

For information about the series and details of previous and forthcoming titles, see https://www.routledge.com/law/series/CAV16

A GlassHouse book

Zoo Veterinarians

Governing Care on a Diseased Planet

Irus Braverman

First published 2021
by Routledge
2 Park Square, Milton Park, Abingdon, Oxon OX14 4RN

and by Routledge
52 Vanderbilt Avenue, New York, NY 10017

A GlassHouse book

Routledge is an imprint of the Taylor & Francis Group, an informa business

© 2021 Irus Braverman

The right of Irus Braverman to be identified as author of this work has been asserted by her in accordance with sections 77 and 78 of the Copyright, Designs and Patents Act 1988.

All rights reserved. No part of this book may be reprinted or reproduced or utilised in any form or by any electronic, mechanical, or other means, now known or hereafter invented, including photocopying and recording, or in any information storage or retrieval system, without permission in writing from the publishers.

Trademark notice: Product or corporate names may be trademarks or registered trademarks, and are used only for identification and explanation without intent to infringe.

British Library Cataloguing-in-Publication Data
A catalogue record for this book is available from the British Library

Library of Congress Cataloging-in-Publication Data
Names: Braverman, Irus, 1970- author.
Title: Zoo veterinarians : governing care on a diseased planet / Irus Braverman.
Description: Abingdon, Oxon; New York, NY : Routledge, 2021. | Series: Law, science and society | Includes bibliographical references and index.
Identifiers: LCCN 2020022920 (print) | LCCN 2020022921 (ebook) | ISBN 9780367403843 (hardback) | ISBN 9780367823276 (ebook)
Subjects: LCSH: Zoo veterinarians. | Zoo animals. | Aquarium animals. | Animal welfare–Law and legislation.
Classification: LCC SF995.84.B73 2021 (print) | LCC SF995.84 (ebook) | DDC 636.088/9–dc23
LC record available at https://lccn.loc.gov/2020022920
LC ebook record available at https://lccn.loc.gov/2020022921

ISBN: 978-0-367-40384-3 (hbk)
ISBN: 978-0-367-82327-6 (ebk)

Typeset in Sabon
by codeMantra

For Tamar, Ariel, and Gregor

Contents

	Acknowledgements	xi
	Introduction Zoo Veterinarians Gone Wild: Meddling as Methodology in Times of Crisis	1
1	"Saving Species, One Individual at a Time": Zoo Veterinarians between Welfare and Conservation	17
2	Fluid Encounters: Aquariums and their Veterinarians on a Rapidly Changing Planet	45
3	Fleshy Encounters: The Corporeality of Bodies and Tools	63
4	Caring and Killing: Euthanasia in Zoos and Aquariums	84
	Conclusion Planet Doctors: One Health from Koalas to Coronavirus	123
	List of Interviews	137
	References	140
	Index	149

Acknowledgements

Thank you to Nili Avni-Magen, Richard Ratzan, Bill Van Bonn, Sam Ridgway, Chris Walzer, Jack Schlegel, Guyora Binder, Shira Shmuely, to Colin Perrin from Routledge, to my research assistant Srushti Upadhyay, and to Istvan Csicsery-Ronay for granting me permission to reprint the three articles formerly published in *Humanimalia*. Thanks also to the Baldy Center for Law & Social Policy for its financial support. I am finally very grateful to my orthodontist, Edwin Tyska.

Special thanks to my family—Tamar, Ariel, and Gregor—for helping me through the long recovery process that ran parallel to writing this book. Healing is an art that requires a lot of practice, and so much care.

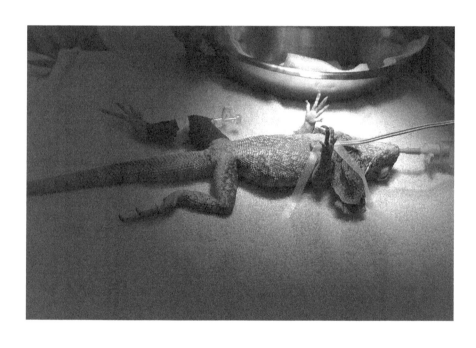

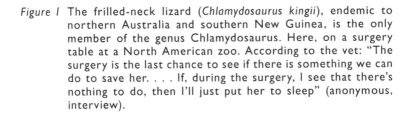

Figure 1 The frilled-neck lizard (*Chlamydosaurus kingii*), endemic to northern Australia and southern New Guinea, is the only member of the genus Chlamydosaurus. Here, on a surgery table at a North American zoo. According to the vet: "The surgery is the last chance to see if there is something we can do to save her. . . . If, during the surgery, I see that there's nothing to do, then I'll just put her to sleep" (anonymous, interview).

Introduction
Zoo Veterinarians Gone Wild
Meddling as Methodology in Times of Crisis

> [A]s long as "disease" is accepted as a natural category, and left unanalyzed, those who talk in its name will always have the last word. It would be better to mix with them, move among them, study them, engage with them in serious discussion.
> —Annemarie Mol, *The Body Multiple* (2002, 22)

Why Study Zoo Veterinarians at this Time?

Despite their centrality to the modern zoo's function, surprisingly little has been written about zoo veterinarians. While there exists a rich social science scholarship on zoos generally and on zoo professionals such as keepers (Grazian 2015), registrars (Braverman 2010), and curators (Berkovits 2017) in particular, zoo vets have received limited attention. *Zoo Veterinarians* attempts to remedy this scholarly neglect. The book sets out to describe the recent emergence of the zoo veterinarian profession and its unique characteristics in both zoos and aquariums. The central insight from this account is that in an age of mass extinction, climate change, and emerging zoonotic diseases, the role of zoo veterinarians is shifting from caring for individual animals to caring for diverse species, resilient ecosystems, and planetary health.

Zoo veterinarians, in other words, are "going wild." Not only are they more involved with direct *in situ* conservation work than ever before, thus extending the logics of zoo animal care to wild animals who were not previously subject to it, but they also bring more wild animals into the zoo as part of extensive rescue and rehabilitation projects. Finally, zoo vets are also heavily involved in programs that release rehabilitated animals and that reintroduce captive-bred animals into the wild. In this sense, the story of zoo vets going wild—in their subjects of care and their motivations, as well as their ethical standards, professional practices, and scientific techniques—is also a story about zoo animals gone wild, wild animals encroaching on the zoo, and, more generally, a wild world that has become "zoo-ified."

Wildlife veterinarians (as opposed to zoo vets) have been around for a while, to be sure. But their work has largely focused on populations, rather than individual animals: they rarely cared for a sick individual or vaccinated wild populations. The extension of the zoo vet's expertise into the wild has thus brought about an intensification of management that traditionally did not exist in this space, such as through husbandry and disease management, and also a mixing of standards and guidelines that formerly pertained only to zoo animals but are now seeping into the wild, including with regard to animal euthanasia.

For this to have happened, zoo vets not only added conservation to their original animal welfare agenda, but many of them have newly shifted their worldview toward an integrative One Health perspective that encompasses human and nonhuman animals as well as ecosystem health. Equipped with scissors in one hand and with novel genetic technologies in the other, zoo veterinarians are at the front lines of conservation medicine. It is not coincidental, I argue here, that these experts are also on the front lines of the human responses to both climate change catastrophes such as the fires in Australia and epidemiological crises such as COVID-19. Their critical expertise in these two seemingly unrelated crises signals that bridging the human–animal divide and understanding fluid interspecies relationships (Haraway 2003, 2008; Latour 1993; Tsing 2012) are instrumental if we are to heal our diseased planet.

My point of departure for this book is what Buddhists often call a "beginner's mind," an open and inquisitive place that allows one to "consider that which is not in our own manner of thinking," and "to come to a place where all forms of inquiry and ways of knowing are seen as having a legitimate place in the cosmos" (Roy 2012, 185). My hope is that readers emerge from this inquiry knowing more about how zoo veterinarians see, think, and operate in their professional encounters and appreciating the importance of their work with nonhuman wild animals. The idea, more broadly, is that alongside the deepening of our own expertise, we ought to immerse ourselves, tinker with, and meddle in each other's professional lifeworlds in order to enrich and enhance our understandings of our place on this planet and help us negotiate the challenges that are facing us, both within the boundaries of our expertise and beyond them. The ethnographic method I have deployed for this purpose, and its intense use of participatory observation and in-depth interviews in particular, are central to my meddling practices here. Such practices arguably democratize veterinary medicine at a time when this scientific expertise is desperately required to mobilize the cooperation necessary to save the planet.

Belgian philosopher of science Isabelle Stengers' ideas on "cosmopolitics" and "meddling" have been inspirational to me in this context. Stengers instructs that just as no living being is like any other, so is every practice unique and unlike another (2005, 184). Calling for an "ecology of practices," she urges her readers to experience "coexisting and co-becoming as the habitat of practices" (184). She further explains that, "Approaching a practice then means approaching it as it diverges, that is, feeling its bordering, experimenting with the questions which practitioners may accept as relevant, even if they are not their own questions, rather than posing insulting questions that would lead them to mobilize and transform the border into a defense against their outside" (184). Later, Stengers refers to this approach as "cosmopolitics"—a term she appropriated from the philosopher Immanuel Kant to "consider that which is not in our own manner of thinking, and to come to a place where all forms of inquiry and ways of knowing are seen as having a legitimate place in the cosmos" (2010, 10). Deboleena Roy, herself a neurologist, philosopher of science, and feminist, laments along these lines that "educational systems . . . have failed to train our students to become proficient in both the sciences and humanities" (Roy 2012, 178).

As humanists and social scientists, we have become well-versed in critical thinking and deconstruction and have, as a result, come to see science as no different than any other story we tell and as no less subjective. Stengers responds to this postmodern tendency, demanding that much more attention be paid to the details and practices of professional forms of knowledge. "The emperor is wearing clothes," she writes. "Everywhere, those experts, bureaucrats, and procedures authorized by science are at work. . . . We have to understand the singularity of scientific fictions and to take seriously their vocation not to discover but to 'create' truth" (Stengers 2000, 44; see also Oreskes 2019). For Stengers, this means not accepting science as an objective truth. She asserts, rather, that "the laughter of someone supposed to be impressed always complicates the life of power. And power is always lurking behind objectivity or rationality when these are arguments used by authority." In fact, the only way to resist authority, according to Stengers, is to concern ourselves with science, to "meddle in what is meant not to concern us" (Stengers 2000, 46).

Zoo Veterinarians is precisely such an attempt to meddle in what supposedly doesn't concern us: the expertise of zoo and aquarium veterinarians. It aims to make visible veterinary practices and procedures that take place behind closed doors and that are perceived as being of no concern to the public, who wouldn't understand them anyway. But as Stengers points out, "the public is not incompetent. They don't need to have their interest stimulated, they only need to be informed and persuaded" (2000, 50).

Why Not Study Zoo Veterinarians?

Far from being a straightforward practice, meddling in fact requires much caution—as I have painfully learned on my own flesh. It was Christmas Eve in 2018, and the zoo I was visiting was quite empty. The staff was planning to leave early, I was told, and so I would only have a few hours of observation. I decided to visit nonetheless. I did not communicate much with the veterinarian on duty that day. I only wrote her how excited I was for the opportunity to observe her work, and how I would be particularly interested in seeing an animal surgery in real-time. It seemed that in my many prior zoo and aquarium visits, the animals scheduled for surgeries would either suddenly turn healthy or they would die, and so the procedures would be postponed or cancelled. In this case, there was nothing scheduled; we were supposed to chat about the vet's work and then head for a round of routine animal checkups.

Upon my arrival at the zoo on that freezing December morning, I was delighted to learn that an emergency surgery would be taking place momentarily. A frilled neck lizard had not been doing well for a few weeks and did not move at all for four days. The cause was unknown, but it was clear that the procedure could no longer be postponed. I was taken immediately to meet the vet so that she could explain what was going on. She told me that when they open the lizard's abdomen, they might be able to discern what is wrong. She suspected that the ovaries were the problem, which is often the case with female lizards in captivity as they do not ovulate. If that is indeed the issue, she would need to pull out the eggs. "If it's her ovaries we can spay her like a dog or cat and it will get better," the vet said. However, she continued, "if the liver is bad, then there's nothing we can do so we would inject some T-61, which is what we use to euthanize them, and then that would be it." The vet further explained, matter-of-factly, that "it may not be a happy ending, but it's the best for her." When I asked what she meant, she clarified: "I think it's an important part of veterinary [work] in general, and zoo vet work in particular, to make sure nobody is suffering. The surgery is the last chance to see if there is something we can do to save her. . . . If, during the surgery, I see that there's nothing to do, then I'll just put her to sleep" (anonymous, interview). Suffering and the elimination of suffering are indeed perceived by many of the zoo veterinarians interviewed for this project as an important, if not the most important, aspect of their work.

At this point, I hesitated. I very much wanted to observe the veterinarian's work in the flesh, but I wasn't sure that I was prepared to observe a death-in-the-making. There wasn't much time to consider, so I asked for permission to video and record, and from then onward I looked at everything from behind the lens. The vet and her intern headed to the nearby room to rinse and sterilize their hands (which takes five minutes, I was told). While waiting, I asked the vet technician—who, as I have learned from my other zoo visits, does most of the technical work behind the scenes (see also Sanders 2010)—what I might expect from the procedure. I had never witnessed a surgery, I told her, and didn't know how I would react. She confided that as the technician who has been at the zoo for the longest time, she sometimes feels sad during surgeries, usually with animals she has known over many years. Then it is harder, emotionally. But since that wasn't the case here, this procedure should be relatively straightforward, at least mentally, she implied. During the entire duration of our conversation, the vet technician was rubbing the lizard's belly with a red fluid, which she identified as iodine.

Many of the issues that I had already observed in my myriad visits with zoo veterinarians across the world also emerged in the few moments before this lizard's operation. The first is the variety of species that zoo veterinarians must contend with and that renders their expertise ad hoc and improvisational. In this instance, the vet admitted that she had never performed a surgery on this species. "But I've done surgery on lizards in general, [and] I don't expect her to be different," she said. As can be seen in the image on the book's front pages, the catheter was injected into the lizard's leg. The vet explained that

> In mammals you would put the catheter in the vein. In reptiles it's very difficult, like human babies, and when it's very difficult to find the vein you go into the bone. The bone marrow is actually as good as a vein so that's why it looks like something is coming out of her tibia, but that's actually a catheter inside her bone. So we used that to give her the first injection and she fell asleep. Now we just put a tube in her trachea and we're taping it to make sure it's not going to move. It's tricky (see Figure 1).

I suddenly noticed that the lizard didn't seem to be breathing. "How do you know she's still alive?" I recorded myself asking, alarmed. The vet replied: "We're going to know in a second, actually, because we're checking her heart. She's a reptile so they can stop breathing and still be alive, which is amazing. And then you can hear their heart." She continued to explain as she started sterilizing the lizard's outer body:

> So, I'm going to administer the anesthesia and do the surgery. Actually, the tricky part is going to be the anesthesia, because she's so compromised that she may not make [it]. Again, it's pretty rare that we do surgery on an animal that's not great to start with. But in this case, this is our last chance.

A few minutes passed in silence. Tools were being handed over, from the vet tech to the vet, and then to the table beside her, and back again. Scissors, pincers, and many Q-tips. The vet slowly cut an incision through the skin of the lizard's belly, and the vet intern hovered over the lizard, helping hold the incision open. The surgery was suddenly well underway, and there was a lot of blood. Everyone in the room was intently focused downward on the lizard's open abdomen, carefully cutting, dabbing, pulling, and cutting again. The eggs were now being pulled out. The pounding of the lizard's heart was projected across the room through a loudspeaker, and it began to feel very hot. I was still wearing the sweater I wore outside, I realized, and the white gown and surgical mask were making it increasingly hard to breathe. I paused to take my sweater off and noticed how dizzy I was feeling. Breathing deeply, I tried to get myself back to the lizard. In the meantime, the bleeding increased, and a semi-transparent liquid also started flowing through the cut. The vet team's movements were becoming quicker, and with them my heart seemed to be pounding faster, too, strangely mixing with that of the lizard. I departed from the table, looking for a place where I could quietly regain my breath and composure. There was no chair to speak of. And then all became black.

I woke up with my cheek on the cold concrete floor. The vet technician was leaning over me, telling me that I was okay and suggesting that I not move until the zoo nurse arrives. A few minutes passed, or maybe it was a half hour. From my position on the cool floor I could observe the vet's back, as she continued to perform the lizard operation with her intern. She did not turn around to speak with me. My face felt like a bruised mess, and there was blood everywhere. The fingers in my left hand were starting to shoot alarming signals to my brain: pain, pain, pain! When I noticed a piece of my tooth outside of my mouth, it dawned on me that this was no small accident. The nurse finally arrived and briefly examined my injuries. She gave me some ice, and suggested that I head back home to Buffalo, where I should probably get checked. You might need braces, she told me when I told her that my teeth were not closing properly.

The nurse stayed beside me until I was able to sit up and leave the room. My family rushed to meet me, alarmed by the news. My eight-year-old daughter's horrified face told me that I wasn't looking too good. I'll spare the readers the details of the difficult year that ensued. I lost my two front teeth; I am still wearing braces and will need to wear retainers every night for the rest of my life; my middle finger is permanently deformed; and my lower lip (which required many stiches) has hard scar tissue at its center.

What am I to learn from this incident? I asked myself this question many times throughout the following year. Is this what happens when a non-expert meddles with someone else's expertise? Is the ethnographer's messing with the black box of medical sciences a dangerous endeavor, and how does one avoid such dangers, while still allowing oneself to be exposed? The year that has passed since the accident contained many doctor visits and waiting room conversations with medical students. During these long waits, I have come to a deeper conviction that what my accident illuminated was the importance of expertise and the need to take it seriously when engaging in interdisciplinary work. In one of our post-accident conversations, my father, a physician himself, told me for the first time about how embarrassed he was after he fainted during a urinary tract procedure in the early stages of medical school. "We get medical students with fainting injuries all the time," I was informed by the physician who inspected me during my nightlong hospitalization in the emergency room.

If my fall was a failure of the cross-disciplinary incentive that inspired it, this book is an attempt to correct this failure by attending to what lay people can and cannot see for lack of expertise, and to what experts can no longer see precisely because of this same expertise. As much as meddling is an essential part of interdisciplinary research—and of any ethnographic project, really—it must be done carefully and with heightened attention to what the expert view can and cannot afford. This is especially true with ethnographies of medical expertise, which reveal the messiness of these highly regulated practices and the gradual disciplinary training that one must undergo to cope with them.

The process of healing, too, requires close attention. Healing ourselves and healing others, be they human or nonhuman, are deeply interconnected projects. A central aim of this book is to broaden our conception of animality so as to challenge the rigid distinctions that separate us from them, distinctions which clearly informed the veterinarian, who did not even approach me when I was lying on the floor beneath her.

How to Study Zoo Veterinarians?

I have been speaking with zoo experts for over a decade now. My book *Zooland: The Institution of Captivity* (2012) includes perspectives from zoo directors, curators, keepers, and registrars. Only later did I realize that veterinarians were almost entirely missing from that account. Because they are the professionals most directly responsible for the animals' health at the zoo, this disregard seemed odd. What happened here? My blindness in this regard was not coincidental, I have come to realize. *Zooland* was concerned with documenting the transformation of zoos from entertainment enterprises into institutions that are dedicated to nature conservation. With their focus on the welfare of individual animals, zoo veterinarians exemplified the traditional animal care model, which did not include much emphasis on conservation.

But this, too, has been changing—and dramatically so. Zoo veterinarians have shifted their focus from exclusively caring for individual zoo animals to also considering, and caring for, the health of populations, species, and even ecosystems. *Zoo Veterinarians* documents this transition in perspective and the ensuing changes, as well as the difficulties, debates, and disagreements among the vets engaged in this process. The book also documents the ways in which aquariums have followed in the footsteps of zoos (in certain instances even surpassing them) and how aquarium veterinarians, too, are realizing the limitations of caring solely for individual animals. Perhaps because marine creatures live in a more visibly fluid environment than their terrestrial kin, aquarium veterinarians have quite quickly come to the important realization that, when thinking about health, one must also think of communities, networks, and the interconnectivity among all forms of life.

Veterinarian Bill van Bonn of the Shedd Aquarium exemplifies this way of thinking. To care for fish, he realized, one must care about their water. His veterinary clinic has thus transformed into a lab: test tubes with green and brown liquid samples from across the aquarium feature in every corner. And after visiting some of his underwater patients, we spent the rest of the morning inspecting various bacteria from those samples through the microscope. More and more of the aquarium and zoo veterinarians I spoke with for this project are recognizing the connection between the micro and macro forms of life and how these underlie individual and herd dynamics. Zoos, too, are coming to recognize the importance of biotic life for their broader institutional setting. In 2018, I visited Micropia—a zoo dedicated in its entirety to exhibiting bacteria.

My interest in zoological veterinarians was thus sparked. And so, after a several years-long break from researching this topic for *Zooland*, I found myself back in the zoo world. This time, I was determined to pay closer attention to aquariums, which were not part of my previous study. Accordingly, in addition to documenting the increasing conservation orientation in the zoo veterinarians' perspective, this book shows the more recent shift of aquariums into becoming conservation institutions. In this sense, *Zoo Veterinarians* is concerned with a double "gone wild" moment: that of zoo veterinarians as a profession, and that of aquariums as an institution.

I started visiting zoo and aquarium veterinarians for this project in 2015. Since then, I have interviewed some 40 veterinarians in accredited zoos and aquariums, including in the United States,

Canada, Israel, Portugal, Germany, Austria, Denmark, Iran, Hungary, Australia, and the United Kingdom. The full list of interviews is provided at the end of this book. Some of the conversations spanned a few days and included on-site observations of veterinary work; others were only a few hours long and were held over telephone or Skype. As with many of my other projects, here, too, the ethnographic process did not end at the interview or with the observation. Veterinarians who asked to be more involved in the writing process, and those whom I invited to read the text in progress or parts of it, suggested points of inaccuracy and ways in which their ideas could be expressed more clearly. In this sense, the finalized text is a semi-collaborative one ("semi," because I still maintained my position of authority and had the final say on what would and what would not be included in the text).

I should emphasize the limits of this study. To speak about zoo veterinarians and wildlife medicine as if they encompass a unitary and global practice is problematic, as it avoids tackling questions about how we should understand localities within the global zoo system. This ethnographic study has focused on a cohort of zoo veterinarians who belong to institutions in developed countries with a specific disciplinary tradition. Although parts of this tradition and its modes of thinking has become globalized, it is nonetheless clear that zoo veterinarians are a diverse group, and that their norms and practices vary according to the local culture in which they practice and its particular relationship to the human–animal divide.

My attempts to include in this study zoo veterinarians from developing countries failed, for the most part, as most of the vets that I reached out to from these countries did not respond. Since I found zoo veterinarians in developed countries to be a highly interconnected community, this inability to form contact with vets in developing countries already speaks volumes about the problem of assuming that the processes identified in this book are shared across the globe. My discussion of euthanasia begins to unravel some of the cultural differences among zoo vet practices, illustrating the extensive variability in dealing with "breed and cull" strategies even among accredited zoos in developed countries as well as between younger and older generations of practitioners. Otherwise, readers are encouraged to qualify the statements made here based on the specific events and voices presented, and to place them in their institutional context, rather than to understand them as grand summaries of veterinary medicine.

Human–Animal Lifeworlds: Between One and Multiple Healths

While meddling in expert worlds is certainly a skill that requires care, meddling in expert worlds that deal with the human–animal nexus demands, additionally, that we pay close attention to the epistemic materialities as well as to the temporal genealogies and ontological classifications that pertain to these specific lifeworlds. The professional experiences and practices that I discuss in this book can be interpreted through a variety of conceptual lenses: posthumanities, political ecology, environmental history, Science and Technology Studies (STS), animal geography, multispecies ethnography, and medical humanities—to name but a few. Within most of these fields, nonhuman animals have recently come to the forefront in what is often referred to as the "animal turn" (Ritvo 2007).

But whereas these fields share an enhanced focus on the animal, each also offers a distinct agenda: political ecologists are more concerned with power dynamics in the human–animal context, geographers with spatial and material dimensions, ethnographers with voice and agency, environmental historians with temporal trajectories, STS folks with co-productions within human–nonhuman networks, and posthumanists with breaking down species-based categories. This is a gross oversimplification, to be sure. I would venture even further to suggest that these various fields strive to explore "nonhuman animals as subjects in their own right and for their own sakes" (Benson 2011, 5; Woods et al. 2018). And they seem to all share a strong desire to break down the nature–culture divide.

Of the various disciplines featured in this book, two have hardly been affected by the animal turn: medical humanities and law. Abigail Woods et al. explain about the anthropocentric focus of medical humanities: "Scholars influenced by the 'animal turn' have not been drawn to study the history of medicine, while historians of medicine have remained largely unaware of the 'animal turn'" (2018, 11). Woods et al. insist with their peers in the medical humanities that "without asking 'Where are the animals?' and 'What do they do?', we cannot truly understand what has constituted medicine in history or what it has become today" (2018, viii).

This book is a grounded effort to support the emergence of a novel field that would expand the medical humanities in nonanthropocentric ways. If we wanted to coin a neologism for this endeavor, we could refer to it as the medical *post*humanities. One sign of the necessity of expanding the medical humanities into the posthumanities comes from the One Health movement. In response to the persistent disciplinary divisions among human health, veterinary medicine, and environmental science, the American Veterinary Association (AVA), together with the American Medical Association, the Centers for Disease Control, and many other health-related institutions, has sponsored the One Health Initiative—an effort to promote work on health across disciplinary boundaries and species divisions. The AVA's 2008 executive summary emphasizes that we are facing "demanding, profound, and unprecedented challenges" associated with a rising demand for dietary animal protein, a loss of biodiversity, and the fact that over 75 percent of emerging infectious diseases are zoonotic (King et al. 2008). The AVA thus calls for a collaborative, holistic, and interdependent approach with an academic presence.

Under One Health, transdisciplinarity is paramount, and meddling is therefore key. Meddling here involves experts in human, animal, or ecosystem health getting to know more about each other's disciplines. The shift of zoo vets toward conservation is therefore not only about adding ecology to their already strong animal welfare expertise. It is also a shift in both worldview and practice from the veterinarian's narrow medical focus on the individual animal body to one that engages holistically to encompass multiple bodies and that which exists among them.

The term *One Medicine* was coined in the early 1900s to highlight the inherent connections between human and animal medicine (Deem 2018, 699). Ninety years later, novel initiatives have taken One Medicine further, into the realm of conservation, resulting in what is often referred to as "conservation medicine." Among the many definitions of conservation medicine, some have offered that it is "a transdisciplinary approach to study the relationships among the health states of humans, animals, and ecosystems to ensure the conservation of all" (699). The book *Conservation Medicine: Ecological Health in Practice* (Aguirre et al. 2002) further defines this new discipline. It argues that, "scientists and practitioners in the health, natural, and social sciences [must] think about new, collaborative, transdisciplinary ways to address ecological health concerns in a world affected by complex, large-scale environmental threats" (Aguirre et al. 2012, 3). Ten years later, Thomas Lovejoy wrote in the preface to *New Directions in Conservation Medicine*: "We have come to understand that the health of humans, animals (and plants!), and ecosystems are all inextricably intertwined. Indeed, given the major disturbance to the biophysical system of the planet itself through climate change and ecosystem destruction and degradation, we also must include the 'health' of the biosphere" (in Aguirre et al. 2012, xii).

Parallel to the rise of conservation medicine, the One Health initiative began to emerge in the early 2000s. Situated mainly within the human-focused medical field, an early definition of the One Health initiative stated that it aims to merge human and nonhuman animal health sciences to benefit both (Deem 2018, 699). However, more recent definitions of One Health include ecosystems and perceive their health as equally important to that of human and nonhuman animals (699). To highlight this difference, disease ecologists working in the field of biodiversity conservation have opted to coin yet another term: EcoHealth (not to be confused with "planetary health," which maintains a focus on human health—only from a global perspective; Lerner and Berg 2017). In 2008, the Conservation Breeding Specialist Group (CBSG) recommended that zoos worldwide encourage their veterinary staff to adopt the integrative approach of conservation medicine and One Health and to direct their skills to conservation efforts at all levels (Vitali et al. 2011, 1–2; see also the CBSG's "One Plan" in Braverman 2015, 204–207).

Alongside the medical humanities, the other discipline that has seen little of the animal turn is law. Maneesha Deckha has argued along these lines that "law is an anthropocentric terrain. Not only is law the product of human actors, it entrenches the interests of humans over virtually all others and centers the reasonable human person as a main legal subject" (2013, 1; see also Braverman 2018b). Elsewhere, I have introduced the concept "more-than-human legalities" to call for legal thinking that is less anthropocentric and more multispecies in its orientation. As I pointed out, "legal scholarship still largely restricts nonhuman animals to the confines of the natural sciences, embracing as truisms their scientific classification into species and subspecies; their sorting into Linnaean taxonomies; their categorization as domestic, captive, lab, or wild; and their relegation as such to particular geographical and emotional zones" (Braverman 2018b, 140).

As in every other medical context, the importance of regulatory regimes cannot be exaggerated, as they dictate—often informally and thus less visibly—much of how the work is performed on the ground. As a legal ethnographer, I am always on the lookout for the "soft" and less obvious ways in which law is imbricated in practices that might seem, on their face, non-legal. The importance of law is especially evident in this book's discussion of euthanasia, where I document the norms, assumptions, and challenges that affect how zoo veterinarians govern death. I am also quite interested in those places that lie outside of the law—those states of exception where the law is relaxed, resisted, or nonexistent.

I would argue, finally, that for a new social order to emerge, we need to think creatively about law. I have indeed suggested elsewhere that: "With the exodus of animals from labs into the social realm, we must envision a new 'parliament of things' that re-orders animals beyond their dualistic classification as subjects or objects so that they may assume a meaningful voice in a new social order. To reflect this novel vision of society, a new way of thinking about law is required" (Braverman 2018b, 140; see also Jasanoff 1996; Latour 2005, 2009). This new legal order—plural, more-than-human, and adaptive—is another important, and thus far quite neglected, disciplinary expertise that must be included in One Health.

Animal Traces: A Brief Structure

Although it is strongly situated in animal studies, *Zoo Veterinarians* is certainly not written from the animal's perspective. It is, instead, an investigation into the perspective of zoo veterinarians. Here, animals perform more as "traces": "those material-semiotic remnants of whatever it is the pursuer hopes to catch, those often unintentional indexes of a now-absent presence" (Benson 2011, 3). Woods et al. explain that when studying these traces, one must ask "not only what they reveal about the health of animals in history and the roles that animals played in medicine . . . [but also] about the animal's capacity to attract human attention, and the relationships that bound them" (2018, 16).

The zoo and aquarium veterinarians I write about here work with—and also co-produce—animals, by configuring them into various categories, roles, and functions. These vets are typically concerned with zoo animals, who are largely construed as distinct and separate from wild animals and also from domestic and farm animals. Zoo animals perform multiple roles: they are ambassadors for their wild counterparts, and they are also research subjects for studies of diseases, husbandry, small population models, and captive breeding—as well as for exploring the efficacy of human–animal and animal–animal boundaries more broadly. In addition to their work with zoo animals, zoo vets also deal with rescue animals who live at the edge of the zoo, as well as with other animals who are either fed to zoo animals, function as their ideal type, or threaten their existence as such. Again, these roles and categories are presented here from the viewpoint of the zoo veterinarian as a means of exploring how these experts govern the zoo's animal kingdoms.

Despite my focus on the vet's very human perspective, I still stress the agency of animals throughout, including in my choice of the words "who" and "her" when referring to animals. Relatedly, I have debated how much corporeality to convey to the readers and whether it would be appropriate toward the animals to display graphic images of them that I, and others, have captured in photographs. The set of images in the book was selected carefully with this in mind, while being critically aware of the difference between animals who still have a face and are familiar to us as such, and those who have become flesh and are thus "deanimalized" (Despret 2016, 83).

The book's four chapters cover different aspects of the zoo veterinarian's work. Chapter 1 documents the ways in which zoo veterinarians care for their zoo animals, and how their focus has shifted in the last few decades from welfare to conservation. Chapter 2 then moves to discuss the history of aquariums and their veterinarians, the unique space they inhabit, and both the challenges and the opportunity that their work provides for protecting the planet's imperiled oceans. Chapter 3 zooms inward to consider the tools and medicines that both zoo and aquarium vets utilize when caring for their nonhuman animals, the different diagnostic procedures through which they produce knowledge about their animals, and their practices of surgically penetrating the animal body. Finally, Chapter 4 examines how and when veterinarians euthanize their animals, and the standards and guidelines that apply to such practices.

The book's conclusion circles back to the failure of my experimentation in meddling, and to the failure of observations by non-experts more broadly, to again contemplate how to "do interdisciplinarity" amidst a world of experts. This exploration is especially acute because

> No one group, discipline or sector of society holds enough knowledge and resources to single-handedly prevent the

emergence or resurgence of diseases while maintaining and improving the health and well-being of all species in today's globalized world. No one country can reverse the patterns of land-use change, marine degradation, carbon release, soil degradation, environmental pollution, and species extinctions that, if left unmitigated, undermine the health of people and animals. Intensive work within each discipline is essential to develop expertise. However, research and practices that bridge traditional disciplinary silos are a prerequisite to resolving the impact of continued human development and growth (The Berlin Principles, courtesy of Walzer).

How, precisely, to bridge the interdisciplinary silos has been the challenge of One Health, which is explicitly, and enthusiastically, inclusive. Animal health experts, human health experts, and ecologists—all have a seat at this table. But social scientists, humanities scholars, and legal experts have, thus far, not been as involved. This book calls for such an inclusion of the humanities and social sciences to build a "multier" disciplinarity of One Health.

Chapter 1

"Saving Species, One Individual at a Time"
Zoo Veterinarians between Welfare and Conservation

> I save species, one individual at a time.
> —Kelly Helmick, interview

So, Who Killed Marius?

On February 9, 2014, 2-year old giraffe "Marius" was killed at the Copenhagen Zoo. Marius was not sick or old. He was killed because he was what zoo professionals refer to as a surplus animal. A member of the reticulated giraffe species (*Giraffa camelopardalis reticulata*; see, e.g., Figure 1.1), Marius was managed by the European Endangered Species Programme, or EEP. According to Bengt Holst, scientific director at Copenhagen Zoo: "our giraffes are all part of the European breeding programme for giraffes, and as a pure reticulated giraffe, this giraffe was one of a European population of a little more than one hundred giraffes distributed over 35 European zoos." "Because he came from a genetic line that has bred very well over the past years," Holst explained, "there was no space for him anywhere in the population, and he was declared 'surplus'" (Holst 2014, 1). In addition to its concerns over limited space and other resources, the Copenhagen Zoo killed Marius to prevent in-breeding within the captive breeding program (CNN 2014).

The ethics of the Zoo's decision to kill Marius have been widely discussed and dissected, both in the mainstream media (e.g., CNN 2014; The Guardian 2014; National Geographic 2014; New Yorker 2017) and in academia (Bekoff 2014; Braverman 2015; McCulloch and Reiss 2016). Rather than duplicate these efforts, I would like to highlight an underexplored detail of this event: the person who pulled the trigger of the Winchester rifle that killed Marius was the

Figure 1.1 Reticulated giraffes at the Buffalo Zoo, 2011. Photo by author.

zoo's veterinarian, Mads Bertelsen. This detail is not incidental, nor is it marginal: the role of zoo veterinarians has evolved considerably in the last several decades and, in fact, they are now the only professionals authorized to conduct serious medical procedures, including euthanasia, on animals at the zoo (see Chapter 4).

The rationale behind Marius's killing is also important: the idea of a healthy genetic population that will be sustainable both at the zoo and as an insurance population for the wild-dwelling members of the species is now the zoo's *raison d'être* and a major goal of the zoo vet's work. Yet while all accredited zoos would agree that no Mariuses should exist in their populations, the means for accomplishing this differ: some zoos ensure that such animals aren't born in the first place, and others kill them when they reach maturity. These variations in approach are the result of different balances that particular zoos strike between the welfare of their animal individuals. The zoo veterinarian is at the heart of the medical and ethical debates underlying the daily operations of zoos, and is central to such decision-making practices—both as the zoo animal's major medical caregiver and as the individual who would typically be expected to execute such decisions.

This chapter explores the changing role of the zoo veterinarian in accredited zoos in certain developed countries, and what these changes tell us about the transformation of zoo animal management. Looking at zoos through the lens of the zoo vet brings to light not only the recent transformation of this institution into one that regards conservation as its central mission (hence, the vet's relatively novel focus on the sustainability of populations), but also the intensification of wildlife management outside the zoo (hence the zoo vet's increased involvement in *in situ* projects and the more individual-based, medicalized approach of wildlife managers). Taking population interests into account complicates the welfare calculus that the zoo vet must consider, making for a much more involved biopolitical project (Braverman 2015). In particular, this chapter discusses how the zoo veterinarian manages the tensions between animal health and welfare, on the one hand, and species and ecosystem conservation, on the other hand. But first, a brief historical note.

The Zoo Veterinarian: An Institutional Context

The word "veterinary" likely originates from the Latin *veterinae*, which means "working animals" (The Veterinary Student 1939, 6). The story of veterinary medicine dates back to Urlugaledinna, who lived in Mesopotamia in 3000 BCE and was an expert in healing animals (RCVS n.d.). The ancient Israelites, Egyptians, and Indians were already familiar with various forms of animal diseases. Moses established a system of meat inspection and Egyptian hieroglyphs recorded the uses of herbs to treat and promote good health in domesticated animals. The Kahun Papyrus from Egypt dates back to 1900 BCE. Vedic literature, which dates from around 1500 BCE, relates that India's first Buddhist king, Asoka, referred to two kinds of medicine: one for humans and one for animals (Canidae 2014). Both texts are likely the first written accounts of veterinary medicine. Much later, Hippocrates (460-370 BCE) described hydrothorax in oxen, sheep, and swine and mentioned the dislocation of the hip joint of cattle following a difficult winter, and Aristotle (384-326 BCE) discovered a few diseases of swine, dogs, cattle, horses, asses, and elephants. Vegetius, who wrote in the 5th-century CE, is generally considered the father of veterinary medicine for his extensive writings on the diseases of horses and cattle (Wilkinson 1992, 13; see also Figure 1.2). Since

Figure 1.2 The title page of the first German edition of Vegetius' veterinary art, from the Wellcome Institute Library, London. Wikipedia commons.

then, there have been numerous literary references to veterinary practices. However, it was only with the founding of the veterinary school in France by Claude Bourgelat in 1761 that the modern veterinary profession was officially born (RCVS n.d.).

If the veterinary profession dates thousands of years back, the zoological veterinarian discipline is relatively new. The first recorded zoo veterinarian, Charles Spooner, was appointed to the London Zoo in 1829. In the United States, the first part-time zoo veterinarian, H. Amling Jr., worked at the Bronx Zoo in 1900. Zoo veterinarians created their own independent meeting venue in the Association of Veterinary Medicine in 1948, and in 1968 they formed their own organization: the American Association of Zoo Veterinarians, or AAZV (Fowler 2006).

The AAZV is the professional association for individuals and institutions who apply the principles of comparative veterinary medicine to zoo and wildlife species. With more than 1,000 individual and institutional members from 60 countries, the AAZV provides advocacy, collaboration, and partnerships for combined efforts in sustaining and improving the well-being of wildlife in all habitats (AAZV n.d.). The members work in clinical zoo medical practices, diagnostic laboratories, reproductive and pathological laboratories, pharmaceutical companies, and a wide range of governmental health and wildlife management agencies around the world. The first AAZV bylaws were written in 1974 and the most recent ones were approved in 2018.

If until the latter part of the 20th century, the health of zoo animals was administered by a variety of zoo professionals (and especially by zoo keepers), contemporary laws and standards have increasingly identified the zoo veterinarian as the exclusive medical provider for zoo animals. According to the 2009 AAZV Guidelines for Zoo and Aquarium Veterinary Medical Programs and Veterinary Hospitals: "zoological parks and aquariums have humane and legal obligations to provide proper husbandry, veterinary medical treatment, and preventive medical programs for their animals" (AAZV 2009, 2). To achieve this goal, "zoos and aquariums in the United States are required to employ an attending veterinarian to provide adequate veterinary care for the animal collection and to assure that certain minimal standards of veterinary care are in place according to the Animal Welfare Act of 1966" (AAZV 2009, 2). Specifically, the Guidelines state that "surgery can only be performed by a veterinarian," and that "all zoos and aquariums must have an on-site area available for minor surgical procedures" (AAZV 2009, 6). These regulatory requirements also establish the obligation of every accredited zoo in the United States to have a veterinarian on staff and frame the work of the zoo veterinarian.

The Guidelines situate the zoo vet as operating within the dual framework of welfare and conservation. Accordingly, Article 2(e) provides that one of the AAZV's central objectives is "to promote the general welfare and conservation of captive and free-ranging wildlife" (AAZV 2012, 1). The combination of welfare and conservation is best reflected in former AAZV President Kelly Helmick's statement, which I quoted in the epigraph, that she "saves species, one individual at a time." Executive director of AAZV Rob Hilsenroth explained along these lines that, "while the effort is on the individual animals, the overview is saving species" (interview). The dual welfare-conservation mission is reflected in the broader platform of accredited zoos (Braverman 2012).

This emphasis on conservation and care has brought about the collaborative management of specific animals among zoo institutions through programs such as the Species Survival Plans (SSPs) in North America and the EEPs in Europe. Currently, there are approximately 500 SSP programs, grouped according to taxa into Taxon Advisory Groups. According to the American Association of Zoos and Aquariums (AZA), each SSP "is responsible for developing a comprehensive population Studbook and a Breeding and Transfer Plan which identifies population management goals and recommendations to ensure the sustainability of a healthy, genetically diverse, and demographically varied AZA population" (AZA 2017). SSPs are collaborative breeding programs that coordinate between all relevant institutions and consider their animals under one managerial platform, which I have referred to as "zooland" (Braverman 2012). A variety of population management strategies serve both to enhance the sustainability within zooland and to create healthy populations for possible reintroductions into the wild. Such collectively-managed populations of zoo animals are often referred to by zoos as "insurance populations" (Braverman 2012).

Zoo veterinarians play a central role in the elaborate collaboration among accredited zoos. In North America, the AZA Guidelines provide the required industry standards for the 230 accredited institutions around the country. According to these Guidelines, a Veterinary Advisor (or VA) must be assigned to each SSP, while the Veterinary Advisory Group (VAG) coordinates between the Advisors (VAG 2001). The Guidelines identify a vast set of tasks for the Veterinary Advisor, ranging between responsibility for medical protocols, health provisions, disease prevention, monitoring and reporting, and providing information on conservation programs (VAG 2001). In certain instances, the responsibilities of Veterinary Advisors extend beyond captive zoo animals to incorporate healthcare for *in situ* animals as well (Deem 2007, 7).

Caring for Diverse Zoo Animals

The modern zoo institution prides itself on caring for a large variety of animals. Accordingly, perhaps the most notable feature of the zoo vets' work is their care for a diverse range of species within the confines of what is usually a small urban space. In the words of Kelly Helmick: "You might see a hummingbird first thing in the morning and an elephant last thing in the afternoon and everything else in between. And you need to know what you're doing" (interview). Helmick emphasized how this diversity carries over into medical practice: "We're the last of the general practitioner. I am an anesthesiologist, I am a pathologist, I am an internist, I am a

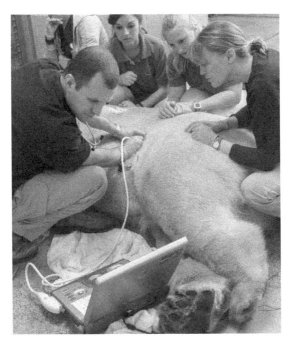

Figure 1.3 Veterinarian Michael Adkesson of the Brookfield Zoo in Chicago performs a routine abdominal ultrasound on a polar bear in 2016. Courtesy of Michael Adkesson.

surgeon, I am an epidemiologist; I am an ophthalmologist, a cardiologist, and a neurologist" (interview).

Michael Adkesson is a veterinarian at the Brookfield Zoo in Chicago. The images displayed here (see Figures 1.3–1.7) relay the vast array of animals he cares for on a daily basis, from polar bears through gorillas and penguins to pangolins and grey wolves. "For some animals, it's very easy," Adkesson told me. But when it comes to other animals, such as aardvarks and kangaroos, "there isn't a close correlation with domestic or human animal data that would provide information on how to treat those diseases, what drugs are going to be most effective, how they metabolize those drugs, and what dosage is most appropriate" (interview).

Leigh Clayton, director of animal health and welfare at Baltimore's National Aquarium, cares for 15,000 animals belonging to 800 different species. The challenge, in her words, is "to take [the] facts you know from one species and then apply them to another species. There is a lot of continuity and similarity." Specifically,

Figure 1.4 Veterinarian Michael Adkesson listens to the heart of a white-bellied tree pangolin in 2016. Courtesy of Michael Adkesson.

Figure 1.5 Veterinarian Michael Adkesson and a veterinary technician examine a Mexican grey wolf pup in 2016. The last five survivors of this subspecies were bred in captivity and their progeny were reintroduced into the wild in 1998. Courtesy of Michael Adkesson.

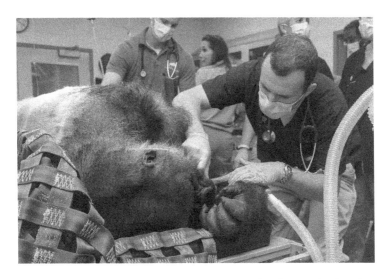

Figure 1.6 Veterinarian Michael Adkesson checks the teeth of a silverback Western lowland gorilla in 2015. Courtesy of Michael Adkesson.

Figure 1.7 Veterinarian Michael Adkesson examines the eye of an Amur tiger in 2013. Courtesy of Michael Adkesson.

Clayton explained how to anaesthetize, x-ray, and operate on a fish, emphasizing that most fish are not traumatized by such medical processes and go right about their day upon returning to their tanks. The difficult cases are with those fish in large containers who cannot be behaviorally trained to respond to the vet. "Schooling fish are hardest to work with as individuals," she was recorded saying (Slate 2017). Octopuses can be quite challenging, too (see, e.g., Montgomery 2015).

The challenges that zoo veterinarians face in terms of the sheer number of species they care for are exacerbated by the lack of medical knowledge about most species, which have a short history of individual care by humans. As Helmick explained:

> There's no book on bear neurology. You can find one of dogs and cats and horses, but nobody wrote the book on how to do a reproductive evaluation on a chuckwalla, which is a type of lizard. So filling those gaps, making those inferences from other species, and making those leaps of faith—and having a successful outcome—is why I like doing what I am doing (interview).

One such leap of faith occurs whenever zoo vets must figure out the appropriate medication and dosage for their zoo animals. Traditionally, humans didn't treat wild animals with drugs: "drugs were made for humans and domestic animals" (Helmick, interview). Even today, there are no medical pills compounded for elephants or bears. To treat many zoo animals, then, the vets must source pharmaceuticals in larger doses and devise clever ways for dosing animals under their care. Helmick described a strategy she used for a hippopotamus who suffered from a skin infection: her pharmacist "came up with something that we lovingly call 'hippo balls'—[which are] 50 grams of amoxicillin in a peanut butter ball half the size of my fist, as opposed to 350 small amoxicillin tablets that require darting the animal" (interview).

At the zoo, safety is always a prime concern (Braverman 2012, 142). This adds yet another layer of complexity to the work of zoo vets. Here, from Helmick's perspective:

> A follow-up visit on a grizzly bear usually requires some type of immobilization, and that's a welfare issue for my patient. That's [also] a safety concern for the staff that I work for. I have to get that animal safely anaesthetized, transferred

across the zoo, usually when the public is there [i.e. during working hours], and safely into my hospital, get all my diagnostics, make a treatment plan [so] that I can administer as many treatments as I can under anesthesia, and [finally] return the animal safely to his bedroom and recover him (Helmick, interview; see, e.g., Figures 1.8 and 1.9).

The zoo vets' medical knowledge draws on, and infers from, medical knowledge pertaining to humans, domestic animals, and animals in the wild. Their expertise embodies the interrelations among these various animals and the need for a holistic approach toward caring for all living beings, while at the same time recognizing the differences between them. The range of species that zoo vets must care for, the lack of medical information about many of these species, and the fact that these professionals are effectively the last of the general practitioners—not to mention that this job is short-staffed and underpaid (and thus also highly gendered)—all exemplify the uniqueness of the zoo vet's work alongside the peculiarity of the modern zoo institution.

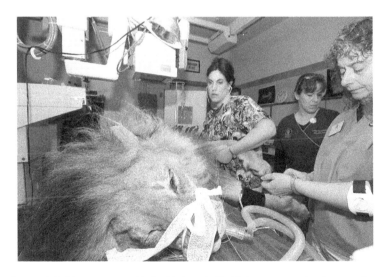

Figure 1.8 Veterinarian Kelly Helmick (left) listens to the heart of an immobilized lion (weighing 178 kilograms) at the Woodland Park Zoo. Courtesy of the Smithsonian's Conservation Biology Institute.

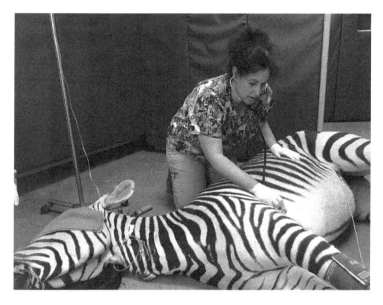

Figure 1.9 Veterinarian Kelly Helmick monitors an anesthetized Hartman's mountain zebra at the Smithsonian Institute. Courtesy of the Smithsonian's Conservation Biology Institute.

Welfare for Whom?

As medical practitioners, zoo veterinarians have an ethical obligation to care for their individual animals. A few questions arise in this context, including what the animal's best welfare is, who gets to make this decision, and how to balance the welfare of different individual animals when they are in conflict. The rationale behind Marius's killing by the Copenhagen Zoo, for example, was that the welfare of his mother would increase by experiencing natural reproduction, instead of the alternative of using contraception medications. Indeed, the most widespread means for reproductive control in zoos is the use of contraception, which is the strategy typically adopted by North American zoos to avoid the need to kill their animals later down the line. Yet, this strategy also presents health risks to the contracepted animals. At the Copenhagen Zoo—which, like many accredited zoos, operates under the premise that surplus genes are undesirable in captive breeding programs—the giraffe mother's welfare interest in giving birth was valued as higher than the calf's interest to continue living.

But who gets to decide whose welfare matters more? Helmick told me in our interview: "I'm a vet, I'm licensed, and I'm accredited. [So] according to the law[s] that govern my role as a vet, I am the animal welfare expert." At the same time, she recognized that "the general public might feel they're the animal welfare experts" (interview). The public outcry over Marius's killing is but one visible example of the "great battle of pastorship," whereby, per Michel Foucault, each group claims to be the sole true caretaker of the (here giraffe) flock and its individuals (Braverman 2012, 20–23).

Alongside the traditional individual-focused welfare calculations, another important normative framework that has been emerging in zoos generally, and that is applied by zoo veterinarians in their work in particular, utilizes the perspective of populations, species, and even entire ecological systems. Marius's individual interest in a continued life, for example, was configured as falling short of the population's interest in sustaining its long-term genetic diversity. Put differently, whereas the exclusive focus of the veterinary medical world used to be on individual animals, concerns about the sustainability of their collective populations that might stump individual interests are becoming increasingly important. Hilsenroth of the AAZV explained, accordingly, that: "The overall goal is to look at what is best for the species that you're trying to save" (interview). The zoo vet must, in other words, act as a Darwinian agent whose primary care is for the survival of the species.

Along these lines, advocates of the ecological approach to zoo animal management have warned that focusing too much on the rights and welfare of individual animals can lead to serious problems at the species level, especially for imperiled species. And since such species are comprised of individual members, so this argument goes, increased inbreeding, disease, and extinction would eventually impact individual animal welfare, too—if not now, then in generations to come. How should we evaluate the welfare of animals who belong to endangered species and who are no longer capable of living outside captive institutions, or without intense human management in the wild? Such difficult situations for the last members of species in existence who have become "captive for life" are increasingly relevant as existing ecological systems can no longer sustain them. I have shown elsewhere that the status of such animals has made a difference to the management of their welfare as individuals—namely, that managing the last northern white rhino in existence is not the same as managing a meerkat or a hummingbird (Braverman 2014). Environmental ethicist Ben Minteer and ecologist James Collins discuss how this sort of differentiated management ends up blurring the *in situ–ex situ* divide. In their words:

> Unavoidable animal welfare impacts produced as a result of high-priority and well-designed conservation research and conservation activities involving captive animals will in many cases have to be tolerated to understand the consequences of rapid environmental change for vulnerable wildlife populations in the field. . . . Inevitably, these changes will continue to blur the boundaries of in situ and ex situ conservation programs as a range of management activities are adopted across more or less managed ecological systems increasingly influenced by human activities (2013, 49).

Zoo veterinarians increasingly find themselves juggling the conservation interests of species, the welfare interests of their individual patients, and the limitations of zoological medicine and institutional practices. So, for example, despite the condemnation by the AZA of Marius's culling, the AAZV's 1998 edition "Guidelines for Zoo and Aquarium Veterinary Medical Programs and Veterinary Hospitals" has already considered that euthanasia "may be necessary for . . . [animals] that are surplus to breeding and exhibit needs" (AAZV 1998, 11). The incident at the Copenhagen Zoo thus highlights the ongoing internal debate within the zoo community, and among zoo veterinarians in particular, about the ethics of caring for individual zoo animals within a conservation framework.

Welfare Hierarchies: Domestic, Zoo, Wild

Although the *ex situ–in situ* divide is becoming increasingly blurred (Braverman 2015) and, with that, the distinctions between domestic and wild animals are also softening, certain zoo vets insist on the continued validity and importance of maintaining these categorical distinctions. Helmick reflected on the complex interrelations between them:

> I do not confuse my pets at home with patients at the zoo. And yet I care deeply for them both and I try to put their interests

forward each and every time. But I don't think people understand that animals serve a purpose, ... and [that] we, as human beings, have a responsibility to those animals whether they're in the wild, in our homes, or at a zoo. Our responsibility to them is different [in each situation]. That's why we do more for an animal at the zoo than for an animal in the wild—in part because we can, but in part because we've taken on the responsibility for that animal—we give it its environment, we provide it with its food, and we darn well better take care of it when it's not feeling well (interview).

Helmick's statement highlights the fact that both zoo animals and the corresponding responsibilities of zoo vets lie somewhere between the categories of wild and domestic. The distinction she makes between these categories is not based on animal type but rather on the animal's institutional context. The same exact fish can be classified as pet, wild, or captive—each with its own baggage of responsibilities. Helmick also refrains from referring to the animals at her zoo by their pet name (something she reserves for pets). Instead, she calls them "patients." The name Marius, she pointed out, was given to the giraffe for internal identification purposes only, and wasn't intended for use by the public (indeed, the Copenhagen Zoo's scientific director never used this name in public presentations; see, e.g., the New Yorker, 2017).

The veterinarian's guarding and reinforcing of the traditional distinction between pet and wild animals correspond closely with the overall mission of the zoo to delineate and reinforce such categorical classifications (Braverman 2012, 69), which in turn aligns with the protection by zoos of notions of wilderness and pristine nature. In fact, the central rationale behind the modern zoo's existence is, arguably, to expose zoogoers to a valued wild nature (Braverman 2012). The difficulties in balancing the various interests and hierarchies among domestic, zoo, and wild settings and animals, especially those who are defined as endangered species, were brought home by a story related to me by Helmick. The story focuses on an instance that involved caring for injured endangered Florida panthers taken from the wild and placed in human care until they could recover sufficiently to function in the wild. According to Helmick, the panthers lived in a five-acre pen at a private facility managed by the United States' Fish and Wildlife Service, which she visited weekly. To ensure that the panthers could hunt after their release, wild deer were placed in their pens as prey. The deer thus served as a tool for the rehabilitation of the panthers, implying that their life as members of an abundant species is less valuable than that of the panthers as members of an endangered species (for a further discussion of the biopolitics of animal management, see Braverman 2016 and 2017). Helmick referred to this as "intensive population management." Here is how she outlined her ethical calculus in this regard:

> The deer cannot escape, [but] neither can the panther. Should [the panther] be allowed to starve? . . . Panthers are endangered—WTD [white-tailed deer] are not. WTD are hunted by humans for food and sport. [Why is] hunting a deer with skill, weapons, and the use of feeding stations to enhance kill success acceptable, but a "welfare" decision [by vets] to contain that deer so that another predator—this time, the panther—can hunt it within a large space, requiring the panther to exhibit skill and ability, isn't? Does a WTD have the "right" to not be eaten by a panther? Does the same WTD have the same right to not be hunted by a human? Humans alter panther habitat to build homes and roads and to plant crops. . . . Does the panther only have the "right" to hunt WTD when a *human* decides that the WTD can "escape" the predator? . . . What are the ethics of releasing a predator back to the wild without ensuring it has returned sufficiently to a level of health that will allow it to be successful in the wild? Should the vet recommend that the panther be fed canned cat food and hope for the best? What are the ethical implications of that? You wouldn't release a WTD back to the wild if you didn't assess its ability to run away; you wouldn't release an eagle back to the wild if you didn't assess its vision and flight capability; you do not return a predator to the wild until you are sure it can hunt. If you can't accept that last tenet and the ethical responsibilities that come with it—then you are choosing to let the panther go extinct because of a lack of human compassion, the presence of human ignorance or bias, or selfishness and an inflated sense of our "ethics" (e-mail communication; italics and quotation marks in original).

Clearly, Helmick's everyday work as a zoo vet presents intense ethical deliberations. And although many animal welfare proponents would likely disagree with her conclusions, no one could suggest that she avoided carefully thinking through the ethical issues. For her, a panther should be fed with wild deer for two reasons. First, the panther was captured by humans and thus humans have an enhanced responsibility for his welfare (this applies to the deer, too). Second, panthers are endangered and thus humans have an additional responsibility to save them, which includes training them to survive in the wild before they can be released. Constructing and negotiating such biopolitical hierarchies among different wild species, and also among members of the same species in wild and zoo settings, are routine aspects of animal management (Braverman 2016) and, as such, are at the heart of the zoo veterinarian's work.

Zoo Veterinarians as Conservationists

The transition of zoo animal management toward conservation is quite recent (Braverman 2012). Like the zoo institution within which they operate, the zoo veterinarian profession, too, has transformed in the last several decades. Hilsenroth described: "It's gone from where we were in the 1950s, when it was mainly emergency medicine, then to preventative medicine, and then [to] sustainability within the zoo populations and, finally, we are now moving toward the sustainability of animals *in situ*" (interview). The transformation in the zoo vet's work, according to Hilsenroth, is not only from an individual to a species focus, but also from *ex situ* to *in situ* conservation.

Generally speaking, zoo vets see themselves as contributing to conservation in three ways: by directly participating in conservation in the wild—or *in situ* conservation; by promoting scientific knowledge about zoo animals as proxies for animals in the wild—that is, using these animals to create databases, archives, serum banks, and, generally, to further veterinary medicine for the benefit of wild animals and humans alike; and by reintroducing zoo animals into the wild (in a way, a more extreme form of proxy, as reintroductions are performed in order to support wild populations—namely, the zoo animals support *in situ* conservation by themselves becoming *in situ* animals). In addition to these three contributions, zoo vets indirectly support conservation by caring for the animals who are then used to educate zoogoers about conservation in the wild (Braverman 2012, 58, 74). In what follows, I briefly explore the three *direct* contributions of zoo vets to conservation.

A growing number of zoo vets dedicate a larger share of their work to support conservation in the wild. Research veterinarian Sharon Deem noted along these lines that, "[i]n addition to the health care provided to captive animals, zoo veterinarians today have a number of roles within in situ conservation projects that ensure the maintenance of healthy and viable free-ranging populations of wildlife" (Deem 2007, 3). Hilsenroth explained that, "to be an AZA certified zoo you have to be doing some kind of conservation initiative or funding some kind of conservation initiative somewhere in the world" (interview). In its 2015 Annual Report on Conservation Science, the AZA noted that zoos spent over 186 million dollars on field conservation projects in over 120 countries, thereby benefiting more than 700 species, 227 of which are listed as endangered or threatened under the Endangered Species Act (AZA 2015, 2).

Veterinary medicine is an essential component of the zoos' *in situ* conservation initiatives. For example, Adkesson of the Brookfield Zoo told me about his work in a protected marine area in Peru: "I've been working down there since 2007 and I'm very intimately involved in a conservation program focused on South American fur seals, South American sea lions, and Humboldt penguins" (interview; see also Figures 1.10 and 1.11). Such *in situ* work is often related to a specific exhibit or *ex situ* conservation initiative, in which the zoo vet is already well versed. Hilsenroth explained, for example, that "if your zoo has some orangutans, you might be doing a project over in Borneo with the wild orangutans and your vet might be going over there twice a year" (interview). This way, *in situ* conservation initiatives simultaneously support and are supported by the zoo's particular strengths and resources.

But working *in situ* also presents new challenges for zoo veterinarians, as the medical resources at their zoos often cannot be transported to remote locations. Adkesson explained that without the very advanced equipment at the zoo, "it can feel like practicing 50 years in the past. So it's a combination of trying to adapt equipment that's used in a hospital setting into a field setting and to make things run [with] batteries [or] off solar panels" (interview). In addition to the technological challenges, there are also the challenges of caring for wild animals in a less controlled environment than that provided by the zoo. Adkesson told me accordingly:

> With wild animals, that animal needs to wake up from anesthesia and recover and be able to be right back in the wild in

Figure 1.10 Veterinarian Michael Adkesson examines a Humboldt penguin at his zoo in 2017. His expertise with this species in zoos helped him when leading conservation programs in Peru for over a decade. Courtesy of Michael Adkesson.

a free-range setting. You don't necessarily have a lot of follow up care or the opportunity to intervene again, so you're really trying to do everything as safely and effectively as you possibly can, while also making sure that the animal is not going to have long term deleterious effects from [the medical care].

Hilsenroth summarized the differences between the work of zoo vets *in* and *ex situ*. At the end of the day, he told me, "*in situ* vet work is much more focused on population health," while in-zoo vet work focuses more "on the health of that individual animal per se" (e-mail communication).

Another area in which zoo veterinarians administer care for *in situ* animals is in wildlife hospitals and rescue centers that are situated in the zoos themselves. Historically, the function of zoos as

Figure 1.11 Veterinarian Michael Adkesson examines two wild South American sea lions immobilized in Peru in 2015, as part of a health assessment project to aid the conservation of this locally endangered marine mammal. Courtesy of Michael Adkesson.

rescue centers has evolved in locations where the central government did not traditionally perform the role of wildlife protection. "The Melbourne Zoo historically has not had a wildlife hospital, but now it is becoming one because more and more people are bringing wildlife to the zoo," Larry Vogelnest of Sydney's Taronga Zoo told me along these lines. "So it's becoming more and more the role of zoos to accept and look after wildlife rescued by members of the community" (interview). "A hundred years ago, if someone found an injured bird or a small mammal, what would be the first place they would bring it to? The zoo!," Endre Sós, lead veterinarian at the Budapest Zoo, said in our interview. Sós also serves as director of the zoo's wildlife rescue center. "We don't rescue game animals [or invasive species]—only protected species," he emphasized. At the same time, Sós also admitted that 95 percent of those protected species are relatively common. "From a purely conservation point of view, it's not important to save 300 blackbirds from a population of 100,000 birds. It doesn't make a difference," he said. "But it does make a huge difference that people develop trust toward the zoo and [toward] wildlife veterinarians—and then you [can] teach them how to protect those species," he explained (interview). This message can become complicated when the public insists on rescuing a non-protected or even an "invasive" or "pest" species. "We don't want to take feral pigeons," Sós told me, explaining their negative conservation value and how they often carry diseases, "which would be a disaster to introduce to a rescue station." But when he has refused to care for pigeons, or other animals like them, people have often become upset. "We try to explain that we really cannot have this animal here because of veterinary reasons," Sós explained. Still, "usually these people don't understand. So we try to find a place in an animal welfare organization. But if we can't, then we have to euthanize them—and that's usually what happens." When you perform this kind of activity, Sós further stressed, "you really have to be careful about the safety of your own collections, too." He therefore emphasized the importance of separating the rescue space from that of the zoo, so that whatever outbreaks or "contaminations" happen with the wildlife there would not impact the zoo animals, and vice versa. In his words: "We had to rebuild our new rescue center a few years ago because the old rescue center was within the zoo, which was really not proper. Now it's at the edge of the zoo, close to the perimeter fence, so it can easily be approached from the outside. We have a separate staff who only works for that rescue facility." Veterinarian Larry Vogelnest of the Taronga Zoo also directs a wildlife hospital situated at the zoo. He, too, emphasized the need to keep the zoo animals separated and protected, while recognizing that "obviously a lot of our zoo animals are exposed to wildlife on a daily basis [as] there are free ranging wildlife species all around the zoo" (interview).

Veterinarian Chris Walzer of the Wildlife Conservation Society was much less excited about the rescue and rehabilitation of wild animals by zoos. He is convinced that such projects end up exacerbating welfare concerns, rather than advancing conservation goals. He explained in our interview:

> It's quite important to draw a clear distinction between rehab work and the classic work of wildlife veterinarians. The public [is often left] with nowhere else to go with injured animals, so they'll go to the zoo. You will never have this problem in Africa, say in Kenya or in Tanzania or in such places that have

wildlife services. They have 50 years of experience dealing with wildlife. They have protocols in place; they deal with this on a daily basis. It's actually countries in some parts of Europe and North America where veterinarians in zoo institutions [perform this rehab function]. The veterinarians involved in such practices, while very passionate about it, are also not very open to reflecting on what they're doing. . . . This is a pity, actually. I mean, you're missing a really interesting part of this profession. . . . The standard veterinary education ignores the concept of selection [and of] evolution, [for example]. So it's quite hard when you come to students in their final year with these concepts to tell them that it is probably detrimental for the population that you're releasing this bird to the wild, [because the bird] potentially releases a package of pathogens into an environment which is completely saturated by the species.

Alongside the zoo professionals who are applying their *ex situ*-based knowledge to *in situ* situations, the zoo animals themselves at times serve as stand-ins for their conspecifics in the wild. The role of zoo vets in this context is to further scientific knowledge about their zoo animals as a way of contributing to the accumulation of knowledge about wild animals at large. Indeed, according to the zoo vets I spoke with for this project, collecting data about zoo animals is important not only in order to manage zoo populations better, but also to better understand their wild counterparts, thereby assisting with the *in situ* conservation of wild animals. Helmick commented, accordingly, how the work of zoo vets both *in situ* and *ex situ* supports and enhances the understanding of individual animal husbandry as well as that of population management. In her words, having a "zoo keeper staff that's knowledgeable and informed about welfare indicators, having those conversations, applying best knowledge—that's going to help some animal in the wild or populations in the wild, at some point" (interview). Here is how Sós of the Budapest Zoo articulated the importance of conservation for his work:

> I was always [motivated] to be someone who was conserving wildlife. And that's the main reason I became a zoo vet. . . . Of course, you work daily in a zoo, so you are involved with a gorilla named X and a zebra called Z. That's not conservation, [but] welfare: you are responsible for those animals and

you like those animals. So that's very important. If you try to see the big picture, then [conservation] is the most important thing—and that's what really matters in the long term. I want to be very honest: I don't like zoos because, somehow, they still lock animals in cages for exhibits. But at the same time, I think zoos are very important [for conservation]. A zoo without conservation is just a commercial enterprise (interview).

Along these lines, certain zoo animals are used as models for research that would benefit the conservation of their wild counterparts. Sós shared with me how his zoo used the relatively abundant Ukrainian steppe viper, which it purchased from breeders for this purpose, to learn how to handle and monitor the endangered Hungarian meadow viper. "When you get the permission to catch ten founder animals of this [endangered] species from the wild and you just kill them within a few months—that's a disaster." The idea of a model species, he explained, is to perform the experimental work on the non-endangered species that is most closely related to the endangered one so that if you do make a mistake, "then it's bad for you and bad for the animal, but at the same time maybe you helped an endangered species." In his view, "This is a perfect example for when [zoos] have to decide between welfare and conversation"— and conservation wins.

Research and data collection that travels along the *in situ–ex situ* divide has already yielded important benefits, Helmick told me. Her best example was the West Nile virus. "It was a zoo vet pathologist who first identified the outbreak," she noted proudly, explaining that the serum samples that she collected in 1982 proved critical for developing the tests used across species. "We helped provide the necessary material so they could validate this test across hundreds of species. It's still the test they use today. We didn't know we would need that sample when we collected it in 1982, but we knew that, one day, that sample from that captive animal was going to serve a purpose for some wild animal or some other program elsewhere" (interview).

Several veterinarians repeated the West Nile virus story as one of the strongest justifications for veterinarian research at zoos. According to Walzer:

> We were quite well-acquainted with this virus in Europe and it didn't really worry us too much, but we'd never seen it in

North America. When the West Nile hit the East Coast of the United States, crows were falling from the trees, dying. At the time, the Centers for Disease Control thought this was the eastern equine encephalitis. But at the zoo we had some emus—Australian ostrich-like birds. And the emus are exquisitely sensitive to the eastern encephalitis, yet they didn't get sick and die. So Tracey McNamara [the zoo's vet] deduced that there is no way it could be this virus, it must be another one. This highlighted the role of zoos as potential sentinel sites because they have these multiple species which have different susceptibilities to wildlife diseases. So they're actually quite good sites for the initial recognition of new viruses moving through (interview).

Apparently, when McNamara contacted the Centers for Diseases Control to report her suspicions, they refused to accept her samples because the samples were obtained from animals, not humans (Khan 2017). This is a perfect cautionary tale about the dangers of a rigid application of human-animal categories.

Vogelnest of the Taronga Zoo similarly emphasized the importance of zoo animals in disease surveillance in the Australian context. In his words:

> We provide data on disease in wildlife to the Australian government. All animals [who die], whether zoo animals or wildlife, have a postmortem examination done and a diagnosis is made. With the wildlife, the results of those findings are fed into a database so that we monitor what diseases [occur in] wildlife. In terms of protecting Australia from incursions of exotic disease, these cases are very valuable. . . . Pathogens are being identified all the time. We've diagnosed several that are not necessarily exotic to Australia, but they were previously unrecognized elsewhere. So it is a very important part of what we do (interview).

Through data and serum, the medical knowledge about zoo animals has seeped into and informed other forms of medical knowledge. "Health connects all species on the planet," Tufts School of Veterinary Medicine Dean Philip Kosch declared in a symposium on conservation medicine (Norris 2001, 7). Much of the focus at the symposium was on the complex problem of emerging diseases. "There are almost no examples of emerging wildlife diseases not driven by human environmental change," one disease ecologist reported. "And few human emerging diseases don't include some domestic animal or wildlife component" (quoted in Norris 2001, 7). Proponents of conservation medicine argue, accordingly, that "just as an ecological perspective can aid health workers in understanding the mechanisms of disease, adopting a medical model can benefit conservationists" (7). Zoo veterinarians see themselves as uniquely positioned to bridge medical expertise, knowledge about zoonotic diseases, and ecological considerations (Deem 2018). As I mentioned in the Introduction, this tri-disciplinary nexus has received different titles and emphases. Once referred to as "conservation medicine," the preferred term these days seems to be "One Health" (Walzer, interview; Deem 2018; see also Deem et al. 2019).

Reintroductions

The third contribution of zoo vets to conservation, and yet another site for exemplifying the tensions between welfare and conservation, is the complex process of animal reintroductions from captive to *in situ* locations. The idea behind zoo animal reintroductions, and a central conservation-based argument by zoo experts in support of housing animals in zoos and aquariums today, is that zoo animals serve as insurance populations—a source for the reintroduction and restoration of captive members of endangered or extinct species to the wild (Braverman 2015, 125–143). Indeed, reintroductions have produced some notable conservation successes in recent decades, including the recovery of the Arabian oryx, the black-footed ferret, and the California condor (see, e.g., Figure 1.12). However, as Minteer and Collins point out: "It is one thing to evaluate captive-breeding programs designed to provide a steady supply of charismatic animals for zoo display. It is another thing to assess those activities with the goal of recovering wildlife populations threatened in the field because of accelerating environmental change" (2013, 47). For these authors, the goal of recovering wildlife populations will "ultimately compel us to rethink our responsibilities to safeguard declining species and promote ecosystem integrity and health in an increasingly dynamic environment" (48).

Moving living organisms to new environments is risky. Some of my past research has focused on the training regimes designed for zoo animals undertaking this transition into the wild (Braverman

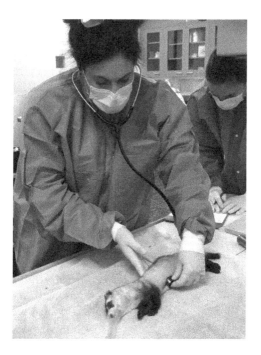

Figure 1.12 Veterinarian Kelly Helmick performs an abdominal ultrasound on an anesthetized black-footed ferret at the Smithsonian Institute. The black-footed ferret is one of the most endangered mammals in North America and is managed through a captive breeding program that reintroduces offspring into the wild (Braverman 2015). Courtesy of the Smithsonian's Conservation Biology Institute.

2014 and 2015). The outlook of zoo veterinarians is slightly different and focuses primarily on biosafety risks—that is, the potential transmission of foreign diseases and parasites. The paramount importance of biosafety in the work of the zoo vet can be gleaned from the following quotation in a veterinary handbook: "the input of veterinarians in reintroduction is paramount. Disease is a major risk factor in captive wild animal management. Reintroduction of captive-bred individuals in the wild could have potentially catastrophic effects when you consider the possible dissemination and risk of an epizootic disease wiping out a population" (Kelly et al. 2013, 165).

The myriad concerns around reintroduction practices have resulted in their heightened regulation. For example, in *Quarantine and Health Screening Protocols for Wildlife Prior to Translocation and Release into the Wild*, veterinarian and chair of the IUCN SSC Veterinary Specialist Group, Michael Woodford, stated: "It is now widely recognized by wildlife veterinarians that every wild creature that is the subject of a translocation must not be regarded as just a single animal but rather as a package containing an assortment of potentially dangerous viruses [and] bacteria . . . any of which may become pathogenic in a new situation, involving stresses [to] individuals in a changed environment" (2000, 7). This approach is holistic not only in that it emphasizes the interconnections between different forms of life, but also for highlighting that what looks like an individual animal is in fact an interspecies relationship, what others have referred to as a "holobiont" (Margulis and Fester 1991).

Conclusion

This chapter has explored the changing role of the zoo veterinarian in contemporary zoos, with a particular focus on North America and Europe, and what these changes tell us about the shifting management of zoo animals toward conservation. In a time of rapid transformation of both captive and wild settings, the role of the zoo veterinarian is also undergoing dramatic change. Whereas traditionally, the zoo vet's main concern was the welfare of the institution's individual zoo animals, it has expanded in recent decades to include not only the diversity and sustainability of zoo populations, but also the health of individuals and populations in their natural ecosystems and, even more so, the health of these ecosystems. The expansion of medical knowledge, especially about disease and its prevention, and the development of complex and integrative *in situ–ex situ* population management strategies, are reflected in and reinforced by the changes in the zoo veterinarian's practice.

The chapter has centered on zoo vets in an attempt to capture the complexity of the animal–human relationship at the nexus of wild and captive settings, at a time when the very survival of many of these animals and species in their natural habitats is threatened. Situated on the front line of care for these animals, both as individuals and as populations, the zoo vet must make difficult decisions about their life, death, and welfare under constantly evolving and rapidly changing conditions. Comparing between, and inferring from, different types of animals and operating in multiple settings, the zoo vet's practices necessitate a complex biopolitical calculus. This chapter has only begun to reveal such biopolitics at the heart of the zoo veterinarian's work, which deserve further scholarly explorations.

Chapter 2

Fluid Encounters
Aquariums and their Veterinarians on a Rapidly Changing Planet

Introduction

The extensive body of social science and humanities scholarship on zoos rarely discusses aquariums. Despite their independent historical trajectory and unique characteristics and challenges, aquariums are considered by many as the younger sister to the more established terrestrial zoo institutions. This perception about aquariums can be explained in various ways: aquariums do not have quite the same controversial colonial history as zoos, they are fewer in number and smaller in size, and they exhibit animals who are less "like-us," and thus not as well-known to science. With the exception of certain marine mammals, aquarium animals have thus rarely been championed by animal rights campaigns, which have tended to focus more on zoo animals such as elephants and gorillas. Of 41,500 species assessed by the International Union for Conservation of Nature Red List in 2017, only 1,500 or so were marine species (Baylina, interview).

Aquarium establishments also necessitate complex physical and technical undertakings: huge water filtration systems, for example, and distinct expertise for handling marine creatures, many of whom simultaneously serve as commercial products in food industries. Aquaculture, which accounts for about half of the seafood consumed worldwide, is the fastest growing sector in the food industry and generates 50 to 170 billion farmed fish every year (Gunther 2018). As one of my interviewees from the aquarium world put it: "it's more complicated to explain conservation and protection and the need for sustainability and constraint in these contexts" (Baylina, interview). Also, unlike contemporary accredited zoos, until recently many aquariums did not hire in-house veterinarians.

In fact, the marine environment was so alien to Western medicine that early veterinarian expertise did not cover it. This situation is rapidly changing. The annual meeting of the International Association of Aquatic Animal Medicine, established in 1968, is now attended by hundreds of veterinarians and includes both marine mammal and fish experts.

This chapter focuses on the novel profession of veterinarians in aquariums, discussing the challenges of this profession and the recent changes it has undergone. I draw on in-depth interviews with aquarium veterinarians in various locations—including the United States, Canada, Israel, Portugal, Denmark, and Germany—to document their unique perspective and the hurdles they face when attempting to manage the health and well-being of marine animals while simultaneously navigating conservation concerns. This can only be an initial study and thus highlights the need for additional scholarly work in the social sciences and humanities on aquariums, their wet forms of life, and the challenges—as well as the opportunities—that their management poses to the human caretakers of this space. This need is especially acute in light of the declining state of extant species and ecosystems in the world's seas. Aquatic species and their watery environments are mitigating and absorbing many of the impacts of climate change and pollution around the globe and have an important role to play in the conservation of our planet, 70 percent of which is covered by water.

Aquariums and Their Veterinarians: A Brief History

The earliest documented aquarists were the Sumerians, who kept fresh water fish in artificial ponds at least 4,500 years ago, and records of fish keeping also date back to ancient Egypt and Assyria (Britannica n.d.). The ancient Romans were the first known marine aquarists: they constructed ponds that were supplied with seawater from the ocean. Although goldfish were successfully kept in glass vessels in England during the mid-1700s, aquarium-keeping did not become well-established until the basic relationship between oxygen, animals, and plants became known in the mid-19th century (Britannica n.d.). In 1853, the Zoological Society in London opened the first modern public aquarium, where it exhibited over 300 marine species in enclosed tanks referred to as the Fish House (see Figure 2.1). The term "aquarium" (from classical Latin: a watering place for cattle) was coined by British naturalist Philip

Figure 2.1 Inside the Fish House, circa 1875, the London Zoological Society.

Henry Gosse and was adopted and popularized by the London Zoo shortly after (ZSL n.d.). Similar institutions were later established in New York City, Boston, Vienna, Hamburg, Lisbon, and Berlin. By 1928, there were 45 public aquariums throughout the world, but growth then slowed down until after World War II (Encyclopedia Britannica n.d.). Today, many of the world's principal cities manage large aquariums. Alongside such public and private aquariums, there are also aquariums that serve chiefly as research institutions (e.g., Scripps Institution of Oceanography) and temporary aquarium exhibits such as those found at world fairs (Encyclopedia Britannica n.d.).

The aquarium veterinarian profession became its own independent profession toward the mid-20th century. Sam Ridgway was one of the founders of marine mammal medicine and also the founding president of the International Association for Aquatic Animal Medicine, established in 1968. A veterinarian and an expert in dolphin biology and communication, Ridgway emphasized in our interview that he does not see himself as an aquarium veterinarian—he fatefully stumbled upon dolphins when working with dogs and supervising food inspections at a military base (see also Ridgway 2008). "Nowadays, [however,] most of the aquariums have vets," Nuno Pereira of the Lisbon Oceanarium told me. "But their presence is not as consistent as in zoos," he qualified.

He and other aquarium vets I spoke with also mentioned that until recently, it was difficult to train for and practice this relatively novel profession (see also LePage, interview). This is how Pereira explained the history of training in this field:

> Back in the days, veterinarians didn't know how to work with fish; they had to teach themselves. There was literature, but no formal education. [So] I went to aquariums in the United States and started to network and we started to help each other. Nowadays, it's better: there are some veterinary schools that deal with fish medicine, so you can start learning this at the university (Pereira, interview).

Notwithstanding the increased opportunities for relevant education, all of my interviewees stressed the still-small number of aquarium vets and the emotional toll that this community's isolation has had on their work. As one interviewee told me: "It's quite strange to be one of three or four persons in this world who can handle this or that [fish] species. It's kind of frightening."

The aquarium veterinarians I spoke with also emphasized the vast differences between zoos and aquariums and the immense challenges of working in aquariums. In the words of Núria Baylina, Curator and Head of Conservation at the Lisbon Oceanarium:

> The pumps, the filters, the disinfection systems—everything [intended] to keep an aquarium with marine species is very comprehensive and is much more complicated than a zoo enclosure where you keep giraffes or elephants. So [aquariums already] start from a totally different place than zoos. The other thing is that in zoos, most of the exhibits focus on one species, while aquariums keep mixed species exhibits. . . . When people go to an aquarium, they want to see the environment, not just one species. It's a little bit different when you go to the zoo—you go to see the elephants and giraffes and you can see them separately. Our theme here is One Ocean. Just because we call them different names, that doesn't mean there are a lot of oceans—it's one body of water. So it's all connected: what we do in one part of the ocean will impact the ocean on the other side of the world. [One last difference is that] you don't eat elephants and giraffes. [But] we are exhibiting species that most people in the world eat (Baylina, interview; see, e.g., Figure 2.2).

Figure 2.2 The quarantine area at the Israel Aquarium in Jerusalem. Photo by author, July 7, 2019.

In addition to Baylina's detailed list of differences between zoos and aquariums, a final major difference between them is that while accredited aquariums in many developed countries are governed by the same industrial standards as zoos and by the same administrative agencies—the American Association of Zoos and Aquariums and its equivalents in other regions—they have not been subject to the same, increasingly strict, proscriptions against the sourcing of animals from the wild, which, for American zoos, date back to the 1970s (Braverman 2012). In fact, aquariums around the globe still acquire most of their fish and, with several significant exceptions, even their marine mammals, from the wild.

Observation as Scientific Knowledge

I already discussed the enhanced importance of vets in zoo institutions and their creativity in adapting medical practices from cats, dogs, and cows, to lizards, birds, and polar bears (see also Braverman 2018a). This is even more the case with aquarium vets, whose everyday encounters include not only fish but also invertebrates, mammals, and birds. How do they care for such a wide variety of species, I repeatedly wondered in our interviews. Veterinarian and director of animal health and welfare at the National Aquarium in Baltimore, Robert Bakal, reflected: "One of my mentors in vet school taught me in dealing with exotic species—and it's very true, all the way down to corals, and for other invertebrates for sure—[that] medicine is medicine and it doesn't matter who your patient is" (interview). As a vet, Bakal explained, he was trained to stick with the procedures to determine the problem. In his words: "The tests for practicing medicine on a dolphin may be different, the diseases may be different, but the approach is still the same: you still do a physical exam [and] you still come up with a list of possible causes and a list of what tests you want to run." Leigh Clayton, Vice President of Animal Care and Welfare at the National Aquarium, agreed. "I call it running the process," she told me in our interview, explaining that: "When you don't know what to do, just run the process. [Whereas] the details when facing a sea star versus facing an elephant are different, the process is the same." Bakal wrapped this up: "I guess if you approach it from a position of being limited, [then] you're limited. [But] I never saw [multiplicity] as a limitation. I actually find it liberating."

While many of the aquarium veterinarians interviewed for this project emphasized the interconnectivity between the myriad animals they care for, they also stressed the uniqueness of aquarium veterinary medicine. Pereira of the Lisbon Oceanarium told me along these lines: "For 10 years I worked with dogs, cats, and some wild animals. To start working with fish—well, it was difficult, because, physiologically, they look like [they've landed] from another planet." Such otherworldliness is precisely what has attracted most of the aquarium vets I spoke with to this specific veterinary orientation in the first place.

The watery nature of the ocean has resulted in the evolution of particular life forms within this environment. The density of water is about 800 times greater than that of air, with multiple implications for structure and size (Balcombe 2016, 12). Pereira explained: "It's not easy to live underwater, so [animals] have lots of strategies to be able to breathe with fewer options than we have in the air." Imagine being a fish, he told me. "Your skin and lungs [would be] in much closer contact with a fungus or bacteria. So they must have a very specialized immune system." Veterinarian Kasper Jørgensen of the National Aquarium Denmark emphasized that these physical characteristics result in the fish's vulnerability. An expert in microbiology, Jørgensen told me that "the most fragile place on a fish is the gills. They breathe with their gills [so] the gills are their lungs. It's like if you'd have your lungs sticking out of the window when driving your car." For this reason, Jørgensen explained, fish are like canaries in the coalmine. "If you have a mixed species tank, you'll see the more fragile fish acting weird first," he told me. To distinguish the "weird" from the normal, the aquarium veterinarian must learn how to carefully observe her medical subjects. In Jørgensen's words: "The thing about keeping animals in this area is [that] you have to look at them every day because, to begin with, you don't know what to look for, until the day that they are acting weirdly. [So I always] walk around. Otherwise, I wouldn't be on top of my game, so to speak, because I have to know the fish pretty well" (interview).

During a visit to Toronto's Ripley's Aquarium, veterinarian Véronique LePage invited me to observe the shark feeding. This hour-long practice involved a meticulous interpretation and documentation of each shark's food intake. "Getting to know their day-to-day behavior, we can more easily identify when something is wrong with the animals," LePage told me. Using straightforward observation methods, aquarium veterinarians—both directly and through other caretakers in their institutions—can learn quite a bit about their "patients"—which is the term most vets I spoke with have used when referring to all the animals under their care, again highlighting the unified human–animal approach underlying veterinary medicine (see also Jones 2003, 3).

In one of his medical observations, Jørgensen distinguished between schooling and individual fish. He explained that for evolutionary reasons, certain animals, including those who travel in groups, will hide symptoms of illness. School fish "do everything they can to not change behavior, like cows. But if it's [an individual] fish in its own environment, we can easily see if something's wrong." This is how the fish observation routines unfold in the everyday, according to Jørgensen:

> From time to time, the keeper will call me and say, "Kasper, let's look at Aquarium 5, something is odd." And then we stand there and we can see [that] they're not moving like they used to. So I take some scrapes. If one [of the fish] is dead then I can do a necropsy. I also have a small heating chamber where I can grow bacteria, or I will send it off to the lab. For the parasites, the best sample you can get is the fresh one, so I will do that myself. Then we'll figure out, "Oh yeah, they had this parasite." . . . But you can also see on the fish that they are not

well, that something is wrong. . . . Maybe it's a fish that lies on the bottom, [or] it's swimming too much. You can see a fish jump out because it's itching from a parasite. You can see them swim more poorly because they have a bacterial infection so their bladder is not working well, [in which case] the scale is a bit raised, you can see it sticking out of the body (interview).

While they may seem incomprehensible to non-expert eyes, fish in fact display a range of behaviors that their human caretakers can learn to observe and then to interpret, understand, and act upon.

Initially, fish care was founded upon group, rather than individually oriented, medicine. According to Leigh Clayton of the National Aquarium, the tendency to study certain animals within groups and populations can be traced back to wildlife medicine, and so the development in wildlife medicine is increasingly relevant also to the care of marine animals. In Clayton's words:

> Typically, no wildlife biologist would treat an individual frog. They would just let it die on its own. But in this situation they did, because there's only fifty of them left. So, you've got this interesting shift: as the [group] numbers go down, the surviving animals become more important as individuals (interview).

Still, Clayton told me that the group or population approach to veterinary medicine, which attaches less importance to the individual animal, is very relevant in the context of aquariums.

Taking from the Wild: The Dilemma of Aquarium Veterinarians

The distinction between wild, farm, and even domestic animals in aquariums is much less pronounced than in zoos. Unlike most exotic animals exhibited in zoo settings, many marine animals are also farm animals. Clayton explained in this context:

> Aquarium professionals have looked at fish more like a commodity than as individuals. [By contrast,] it's been a really long time since lions or elephants were considered a commodity. . . . When you're talking about an individual sand tiger [shark], [that's one thing,] but when you're talking about 500 kilograms of fish from Chesapeake Bay that has millions of

them, [that's a very different ballgame.] It's not that people don't care; they do care, desperately. But there hasn't been the pressure, internally or externally, to care about every *single* fish (interview).

Along these lines, aquarium professionals have told me that it has been difficult to explain to the public why they should care about saving the same herring or lobster that they would later find on their plate. Clayton stressed, however, that this situation is rapidly changing as fish are increasingly perceived by the public as worthy subjects of individualized attention.

Two of the questions that have been more or less settled in the zoo conservation context for the last few decades are whether to take animals from the wild (absolutely not) and whether to reintroduce wild animals back into the wild (a worthy but challenging endeavor). For the most part, aquariums have been answering these questions differently than zoos, although this, too, is changing (Figure 2.3). "We talk about it all the time, that aquariums are 20 years behind," Clayton responded when I asked her how aquariums compare with zoos, especially in terms of their role in conservation.

Figure 2.3 A sea lion show at the Lisbon Zoo. Many aquariums have terminated such shows for what some perceive as their problematic anthropomorphizing of marine animals. Photo by author, July 9, 2018.

54 Fluid Encounters

Most marine animals held in aquariums are wild-caught. The United States imports 11 million tropical fish each year, who live in an estimated 2 million saltwater aquariums across the country, while the global saltwater fish trade nets as much as 330 million dollars annually (Weber 2015). The New England Aquarium's Director of Ocean Sustainability Science, Michael Tlusty, and the institution's research scientist, Andy Rhyne, told me about the damages that the ornamental and pet fish industry—with its indiscriminate strategies of cyanide fishing and bottom trawling—has wrought upon fish, marine mammals, and their wet ecosystems. At the same time, they also emphasized that this sorry situation should not translate into a complete ban on taking aquatic creatures from the wild. In fact, they have been arguing that purchasing wild-caught corals is more conservation-friendly than buying corals from farms and aquarist tanks (Braverman 2018a, 2019a, 2019b; see also Figure 2.4).

Similar to the debates about whether to source corals from the wild, the debates about whether to source fish from the wild are ongoing and, as is often the case with animal-related issues, can be quite heated. While the vast majority of aquariums continue this practice, many have become much more selective about regulating

Figure 2.4 Tanks behind the scenes in the New England Aquarium, Boston, MA. Photo by author, May 11, 2016.

how their fish are captured so as to minimize harm to both the fish and their habitat. Indeed, the estimated mortality in the reef-to-retail chain ranges from 10 to as high as 80 percent for different marine species. Transport practices for the ornamental and pet industry have included starving fish so that they do not foul their water, subjecting them to fluctuating temperatures, holding them in water of poor quality, and exposing them to harsh medications (Algae Barn n.d.). As a result, certain states, such as Hawai'i, have introduced laws requiring higher standards for fish transport (Weber 2015).

Although most aquarium animals are still acquired from the wild (Parsons, interview), aquariums distinguish themselves from the pet and ornamental industries in the way they obtain their animals. Leah Neal, formerly Director of Husbandry at the Ripley's Aquarium in Toronto, Canada, described her aquarium's increased precautions with regard to fish sourcing:

> We have vendors that we go through and we know their supply chain. So we're not going to the Mom and Pop [pet] shops online. We also collect at the Florida Keys, where we have a "no-hands" rule: we use nets and try not to handle the fish at all. We have permits, but [in addition], when we decide if to take small versus big animals, we [opt to] leave the reproducing ones on the reefs. That way, we are in control. In Baltimore [and also] in [the] New England [Aquarium] they go to the Bahamas once a year. Out in the West Coast, they [also] do their own collecting. We like to know that we're handling those animals from start to finish (interview).

Relatedly, and although this is also changing rapidly, most animal populations in aquariums are not part of captive breeding programs. The aquarium vets I interviewed explained this by pointing to the technical and scientific challenges of captive breeding marine mammals and fish, also emphasizing the high costs of these endeavors. Jørgensen of the National Aquarium Denmark and Copenhagen Zoo veterinarian Kathryn Perrin discussed this point when I interviewed them jointly in Copenhagen:

> KJ: In Holland [there's] an aquarium that says "we do not receive animals from the wild." That is very cool, except they always ask us if we have any animals. And for them it's not

a problem to receive our animals that we retrieved from the wild, and then it's as if they didn't take them from the wild.

KP: It would be really cool if you had an aquarium that genuinely did not source animals from the wild. That would be so cutting-edge.

KJ: Yeah, I think that would be very nice, except it would be stupid to not just bring the herring from out here because there's a lot of them—there's really a lot.

This brief exchange reveals a fundamental divide between veterinarians across distinct institutions and geographies, and especially between zoo vets and certain aquarium vets. Whereas both zoo vets and an increasing number of aquarium vets, represented here by Perrin, categorically prefer captive breeding over taking animals from the wild, many aquariums have been promoting a less categorical approach, represented here by Jørgensen. In his view, certain fish can be sustainably harvested for aquariums from the wild, similar to their harvesting for the food industry.

A related issue has to do with the transition of animal bodies from the wild into captivity. Those animals who are subject to this transition are exposed to a variety of challenges, Jørgensen explained. He provided an example from the world of sharks to illustrate some of the veterinary problems that occur as a result of the transition. In many public aquariums, sharks are an essential part of the collection and represent one of the biggest draws for the public (Grassmann et al. 2017). But the method of capturing them from the wild in certain locations involves the unregulated application of certain antibiotics, which introduces a host of risks not only for the specific fish but also for aquariums. In his words:

> The [Indonesian] fishermen [who] earn their money catching sharks keep them in small tanks and ship them out to different aquariums. Most of them keep the fish alive in these small places by adding a lot of antibiotics. When I receive a shark from Indonesia and they get a bacterial disease that needs to be treated, they are always resistant to Enrofloxacin, which is because the fishermen just poured it into the water. I am sure of it. And Enrofloxacin is supposed to be a reserved antibiotic. It shouldn't be used as a first line antibiotic—you should save it for the infections you really need it for. It's very commonly used in exotic species because it's safe and it works (interview).

As a result of these problematic capture practices by the Indonesian fishermen, the recently acquired aquarium sharks could no longer be treated properly. "That shark is gone," as Jørgensen put it. He commented, further, that the aquarium's human divers could get infected by the same resistant bacteria, which is likely to then infiltrate the aquarium's water system. To avoid such messy zoonotic transmissions, the National Denmark Aquarium no longer obtains sharks from Indonesia, instead acquiring them from Kenya. "We've been down there and we've seen the facilities and I've written the treatment protocols and told [the fishermen] what to do and how we would like the fish we are getting." Rather than deciding to stop taking fish from the wild altogether, even the conservation- and welfare-minded aquariums often prefer to adjust the protocols so as to more safely and sustainably continue taking marine animals from the wild.

At the same time, captive breeding is becoming increasingly feasible for a growing number of aquatic species. This feasibility is most apparent with regard to marine mammals such as dolphins and whales (The Dodo 2016), as well as certain shark and ray species (Bakal, interview). Whereas captive breeding programs have existed in zoos since the late 1970s, public aquariums in Europe established their initial two marine fish studbooks and collaborative breeding programs only in 2007—first for zebra sharks (*Stegostoma fasciatum*) and then for blue-spotted stingrays (*Taeniura lymma*). Núria Baylina is Curator and Head of Conservation at the Lisbon Oceanarium and the studbook keeper for the blue-spotted stingray breeding program. She told me in our interview that the rays' captive population of 130 individuals is currently managed among various European aquariums with an eye toward conservation. "Ten years ago, we didn't know much about them and we couldn't figure out how to breed them," she said. "Now, we're in the second or third [captive bred] generation. Compiling this information and using this network really helps to develop our knowledge about the species."

From Baylina's perspective, the knowledge developed about captive marine animals is valuable for the conservation of their wild conspecifics, especially because biologists are usually unable to monitor the latter closely in the oceans. In the case of the blue-spotted stingrays, captive breeding in aquariums will likely also reduce pressure on the wild populations from hobby aquarists. Furthermore, according to Baylina: "if this species will become threatened or endangered, we [would] have the knowledge to [embark on a] reintroduction program. So we'll be prepared if we need to use these techniques for the species in the future." She summarized: "A lot of [lay] people think we just keep the species for them to see, but that's not the main goal of [today's] aquarium." In the United States, the American Association of Zoos and Aquariums recently established the program SAFE: Saving Animals from Extinction," which "takes a collaborative approach to recognize, promote and bolster conservation efforts for selected species" (AZA n.d.). Four of the five focal species or species groups selected for 2015 were aquatic: African penguins, sea turtles, sharks, and vaquitas. This again goes to highlight the critical state of ocean biodiversity and the importance of aquariums for marine conservation.

Additional changes are also underway for marine management in aquariums. Some institutions, such as the National Aquarium in Baltimore and the Shedd Aquarium in Chicago, have recently announced that they will no longer exhibit dolphins and orcas and that they will send captive animals from these taxa to semi-wild sanctuaries. The Lisbon Zoo's vet assured me along these lines that: "In Europe, you won't see a [newly] wild-caught dolphin in any accredited zoo or aquarium; not even one" (Bernardino, interview). At the same time, veterinarians have called for the captive propagation of certain marine animals, such as the endangered river dolphin, with the underlying assumption that suffering captivity is better than suffering extinction (Ridgway et al. 1989; see also Braverman 2014).

Reintroducing Marine Animals

While many aquarium vets admit that they lag behind zoos in that they still capture animals from the wild and in their technical capacity to breed animals in captivity, they also highlight that aquariums are particularly well-suited for moving animals in the other direction: from zoos back to the wild. Under certain circumstances, conservation professionals define this movement as a "reintroduction" (Braverman 2015). Perrin of the Copenhagen Zoo admitted that "every vet dreams about being involved with reintroductions and making an impact."

The central reasoning behind zoo animal reintroductions is the conservation of endangered species. Jørgensen is convinced that in light of the degrading state of marine ecosystems due to pollution, overfishing, ocean acidification, and global warming, aquariums must urgently assume a novel institutional role as the new Noah's Arks. He explained in the context of sea otters, for example, that the captive populations are a "backup for the world." So "if catastrophe hits Alaska, we will have fertile animals, and we will know how to breed them." (He lamented, however, that the existing legal regime prohibits his aquarium and others from breeding otters.) Similarly, "with corals, aquariums are the backup," he told me. "And the way that the world is going now, at some point we will need this backup." As for fish, in terms of inbreeding and genetic diversity, they are better suited for captive breeding than any other taxa, Jørgensen said. "With fish you can go through a lot of generations of inbreeding with no problem." As mentioned above, aquariums are developing the capacity to breed marine animals in captivity. But a crucial component of the aquariums' function as Noah's Arks will be their ability to then reintroduce these animals to ocean locations. While reintroductions have been a challenging undertaking with regard to many terrestrial animals (Braverman 2015), fish are much easier. Jørgensen told me, accordingly, that "you can just take two hundred fish and put them out where they came from, even after three generations [in captivity], and they will live perfectly."

Despite their potential importance for species conservation, reintroductions have been legally prohibited in many countries, mostly due to concerns over pathogens and genetic "pollution." Still, Jørgensen strongly believes that reintroductions will be inevitable and that aquariums should be investing in both medical veterinary knowledge and husbandry skills to execute them (see also Stokstad 2013). In his words:

> Aquariums should work toward releasing the animals that we reproduce instead of euthanizing them. It's fine for me to put them down [i.e., euthanize them, IB] if there are too many, but I'd rather just put them out in the wild. Because [we] can easily do that. You have [to undergo] some very strict quarantine procedures but . . . it's possible. In Madagascar, for example, all the riverbeds are drying out and getting polluted. We have some cichlid [fresh water fish, IB] from Madagascar that are going to be extinct in the wild in a few years. We are the only aquarium in Europe keeping these fish and we are trying to breed them just in case some government at some point allows us to let them out again (interview).

"I really think we should reintroduce a lot more fish, and make it possible to do that," Jørgensen said, and a growing number of his cohorts in aquariums would agree. In their view, contemporary aquariums should perform a much more active role in marine animal conservation and, correspondingly, aquarium veterinarians should be better educated in the relatively new field of conservation medicine (Aguirre 2002, viii).

Do Fish Feel Pain?

The question of whether certain animals do, or do not, feel pain has substantial implications for the everyday work of veterinarians. In the aquarium context, a fierce debate is ongoing about whether or not fish—a taxon that includes some 34,000 species (FishBase 2018)—feel pain. Veterinarian Kathryn Perrin of the Copenhagen Zoo considered aloud in our interview: "Of course the elephant feels pain, but does a [fish] feel pain?" She immediately replied that, "Personally, I feel that there's pretty good evidence that, sadly, animals from fish upwards feel pain. There is also increasing evidence that it's more difficult with invertebrates to distinguish pain versus reflex."

And yet, the science is still divided on this topic. Perrin explained that the crucial distinction here is between nociceptive reflex and cognitive pain, whereby "there's some sort of mental process about it being a negative experience." "If you don't *perceive* it as painful, [then] it's not the same thing," she said. The question is how to know and quantify these responses in animals, who cannot inform us about their feelings in ways that we can easily comprehend and measure (see also Dror 1999). "You can't really measure pain in animals because pain is the emotion associated with a negative stimulus," Perrin continued. Instead, "you apply a stimulus that you assume is painful—heat, electric shock, or a chemical stimulus—to try and replicate a painful stimulus in a repeatable way that's consistent with, but [still] very different from, pain."

With respect to fish, the assumption for quite some time has been that they don't feel pain. In their 2014 article "Can Fish Really Feel Pain," James Rose and his colleagues reviewed studies that concluded that fish feel pain and claimed that there were deficiencies in the methods used for pain identification, concluding that "claims that fish feel pain remain unsubstantiated." They wrote:

In contrast, an extensive literature involving surgeries with fishes shows normal feeding and activity immediately or soon after surgery. . . . We evaluate recent claims for consciousness in fishes, but find these claims lack adequate supporting evidence, neurological feasibility, or the likelihood that consciousness would be adaptive. Even if fishes were conscious, it is unwarranted to assume that they possess a human-like capacity for pain (Rose et al. 2014, abstract).

The same article concluded that, "Overall, the behavioral and neurobiological evidence reviewed shows fish responses to nociceptive stimuli are limited and fishes are unlikely to experience pain" (2014, abstract). In his article "Why Fish Do Not Feel Pain" (2016), Australian neuroscientist Brian Key agreed with these statements. "It doesn't feel like anything to be a fish," he added elsewhere (cited in Safina 2018).

By contrast, Jonathan Balcombe's *What a Fish Knows: The Inner Lives of Our Underwater Cousins* spoke to the sentient and rich mental life of fish: "Scarcely a week now passes without a revealing new discovery of fish biology and behavior . . . that defy the human conceit that fishes are dim-witted pea brains and slaves to instinct. Fishes are not just sentient, but aware, communicative, social, tool-using, virtuous, even Machiavellian" (2016, 19). Similarly, oceanographer Sylvia Earle has stated that "I find it astonishing that many people seem shocked at the idea that fish feel. The way I see it, some people have wondrous fish-like characteristics—they can think and feel!" Fish "have senses we humans can only dream about," Earle continued. "Try to imagine having taste buds all along your body. Or the ability to sense the electricity of a hiding fish. Or eyes of a deep sea shark" (cited in Safina 2018). Engaging with this question from a different perspective, recent studies have shown that pain in humans is a very elusive phenomenon (Bourke 2014; Moscoso 2012; Wailoo 2014).

Whereas the aquarium veterinarians I interviewed all admitted that they do not have an unequivocal scientific answer to the question of whether or not fish feel pain, they have nonetheless opted to work under the premise that fish do, either because they experience this to be true from their everyday practice of caring for fish, or due to the precautionary principle. Perrin told me along these lines that "Most zoo vets err on the side of caution: if you suspect there's pain, then you should be doing something about it." Ripley's veterinarian LePage was even more explicit: "That there is still a debate about this topic is totally baffling to me. I just don't get the obsession about sentience in this context. To me it is obvious: Fish feel pain!" (interview).

Conclusion: Fluid Futures

This chapter has sketched a portrait of the modern aquarium through the eyes of its veterinarians, a small but rapidly growing, and quite influential, professional cohort. With their feet in several worlds, aquarium veterinarians must balance their medical training and animal welfare sensibilities with the specific nature of the marine animals under their care, alongside the understanding of these animals' increasingly important role in ocean conservation. For these professionals, the rights-welfare-conservation approaches to animal care are not abstract ideas but real-life situations that dictate their everyday practices of caring for marine animals. As one aquarium veterinarian told me in a statement that is also relevant in the zoo context: "These animals pay a price to be here. The price is [that] they don't have freedom. What we must give them in return are the best conditions possible—like medicine, surgery, et cetera—which they wouldn't get in the wild."

Chapter 3

Fleshy Encounters
The Corporeality of Bodies and Tools

> For materiality is always something more than mere matter: an excess, force, vitality, relationality, or difference that renders matter active, self-creative, productive, unpredictable.
> —Diana Coole and Samantha Frost, *New Materialisms*, 9

Veterinary Spaces and Materialities: An Introduction

To the untrained eye, veterinary hospitals in zoos and aquariums look strikingly alike, and not much different from, human hospitals. When browsing through the images displayed in this book, one might consider the choice of paint color, the white neon lighting, and the sterile feel of exposed surfaces. There are also visible variations in the types of equipment and tools that inhabit these veterinary spaces (see, e.g., Figures 3.1 and 3.2). The pharmacy, with its myriad cabinets of boxed and bottled drugs, is either situated in a separate room, as in the Berlin and Lisbon Zoos (see, e.g., Figure 3.3), within the surgical rooms, as in the Shedd Aquarium—or in both, as in SeaWorld. Terrestrial zoos with dangerous exotic animals are required to maintain shotguns and tranquilizers in working condition in case of animal escape or other emergencies.

At the aquarium, the space of the exhibit is uniquely defined by water (see, e.g., Figures 3.4 and 3.5).

Watery Environments

> The pumps, the filters, the disinfection systems—everything [intended] to keep an aquarium with marine species is very comprehensive, and is *much* more complicated than an enclosure where you keep giraffes or elephants.
> —Nuria Baylina, interview

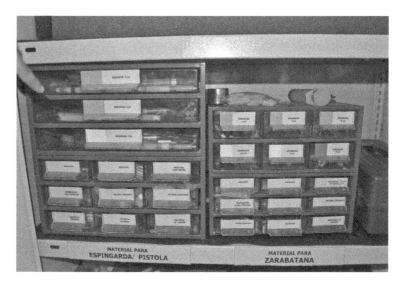

Figure 3.1 Lisbon Zoo's tranquilizer drawers, *espingarda pistola* (Portuguese for "shotguns") and *material para zarabatana* (anesthesia serum for the syringes). Photo by author, July 9, 2018.

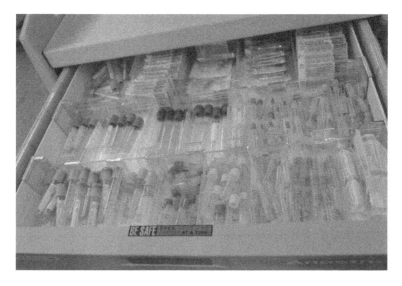

Figure 3.2 Tubes at the veterinary clinic at the SeaWorld Park in Orlando, Florida. Photo by author, October 11, 2019.

Fleshy Encounters 65

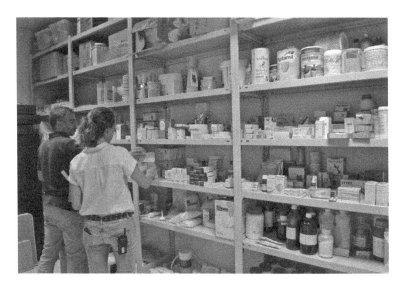

Figure 3.3 Lisbon Zoo's Veterinarian Rui Bernardino and his colleague at the zoo's pharmacy. Photo by author, July 9, 2018.

Figure 3.4 Water pumps are exhibited to the public at Ripley's Aquarium in Toronto, Canada. This aquarium maintains 5.2 million liters of water, which are "about 25,000 bathtubs!" (Ripley's Aquarium, n.d.). Photo by author, November 22, 2018.

Figure 3.5 Water tanks—a view from the staff restricted area. The public exhibit is located below the staff access space. National Aquarium Denmark, Den Blå Planet. Photo by author, July 30, 2018.

Just as a fish is not a fish is not a fish, water is not water is not water. Whereas some aquariums pump and treat water from open sources, others utilize tap water and process it within their own aquarium to produce saline and fresh water. Each of these methods comes with its own challenges and costs.

Either way, there is a growing realization on the part of aquarium veterinarians that the health of their visible macroorganisms is highly dependent on the health of their invisible (to the naked human eye, that is) microorganisms. While not referring to bacteria as their "patients"—not yet, at least—veterinarians have come to understand that diverse and balanced microbial communities in their aquarium's waters are crucial for healthy microbiomes on and within their animals. For far too long, the ideal was a sterile water system, veterinarian Bill Van Bonn, Vice President of Animal Health at the Shedd Aquarium, told me in our interview. This ideal, encoded into USDA standards and inspected by federal agencies and industry associations alike, is now being reconsidered. The new question is: "How clean is *too* clean for aquarium animals?" According to Chrissy Cabay, Director of Shedd Aquarium's

Microbiome Project, this is perhaps the most important question that marine animal experts must contend with if they wish to provide a healthy environment for the aquarium animals under their care (interview).

Alongside his dealings with massive beluga whales, sharks, and rays, Van Bonn's daily work thus requires acquainting himself with, and caring for, the tiny fungal, bacterial, and archaean life thriving in his institution's marine environment (the veterinarians I spoke with admitted that they still know very little about viruses). We spent a large chunk of our morning peering through a microscope at the array of microbes in cultures taken from different parts of the aquariums' animals and waters: the nose of a dolphin, the shell of a turtle, a swab from a yellow stingray, and water samples from various exhibits (see, e.g., Figures 3.6 and 3.7). Van Bonn consistently stressed "the value of basic science work enabled by the privilege of having the animals in our care." He referred to this work as "science beyond conservation." When I asked him to explain, he said: "The idea of simply knowing nature is an important and valuable function of zoos and aquaria that is not recognized enough" (e-mail communication). Some have argued that

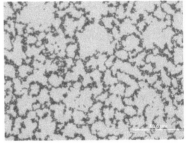

Figures 3.6 and 3.7 Aquarium-dwelling bacteria. According to Shedd Aquarium's veterinarian Bill Van Bonn: "These two types of bacteria represent two very different morphologies of commonly found aquatic bacteria. Filamentous bacteria are sometimes associated with skin infections in a variety of fishes, and enterococci can sometimes cause septicemia—an infection that spreads through the bloodstream. As with all bacteria, their mere presence is not the problem. Conditions must be right to favor them" (interview). Courtesy of ©Shedd Aquarium.

this idea is especially acute when it comes to microbiome management (West et al. 2019). If the zoo veterinarian described thus far has moved beyond animal welfare to the realm of conservation management, then the emerging vet not only connects between the two, but also recognizes the fluid boundaries between lively bodies and their environments.

Techniques and Technologies, Instruments and Tools

> When we come under the spell of the deeper domain of techniques, its economic character and even its power aspect fascinate us less than its playful side. . . . This playful feature manifests itself more clearly in small things than in the gigantic works of our world.
> —Ernst Junger, *The Glass Bees*, 132

> Acrouch, strung, the surgeon is one with his instrument; there is no boundary between its metal and his flesh.
> —Richard Selzer, *The Art of Surgery*, 21

Since most medical and surgical equipment is not designed with nonhumans in mind, and that which is designed for nonhumans focuses mainly on farm and domesticated animals, zoo and aquarium veterinarians must be highly creative in adjusting existing equipment to the particular nature and needs of the wild animals under their care. This creativity manifests in elevators and tables that fit a variety of body sizes and weights, inhalation machines large enough for whales or elephants, and transportable ultrasound and laparoscopy technology. Drug quantities and concentrations must also be adjusted for myriad body sizes and conditions.

During my observations of zoo vets in surgery rooms, I was particularly drawn to the multitude of scissors they use. Accustomed to one or two types, I found the vast array of scissors on display enchanting (see, e.g., Figure 3.8). Perhaps another reason for my enchantment was the realization that such scissors are used accurately and intently to cut the flesh of living organisms. Something about the mundaneness of this tool explicates the unique variety of bodies, tissues, and issues that veterinarians must contend with when dealing with such a diverse range of nonhuman animal bodies.

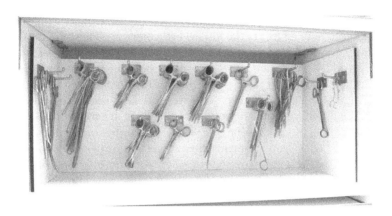

Figure 3.8 Surgical scissors at the Lisbon Zoo. Photo by author, June 2018.

Lydia Staggs, senior veterinarian at SeaWorld, described the function of scissors, as well as an additional two types of mundane technical tools used by vets: hemostats and forceps. "Forceps are for gripping things," she explained. "You don't want to use your fingers, you need to use an extension—so you have different forceps for that." "Why not use your fingers?" I wondered. "Well, it's not as good sometimes," she responded, laughing, perhaps implying that there needs to be a separation between one body and the other. Staggs also noted the importance of accuracy in surgical procedures on living animals: the thin interconnective tissues are so sensitive to the touch that the less you disturb them, the better (apparently, the process is quite different in necropsy procedures, which are mandatory for every animal who dies at the facility).

"The hemostat is for clamping," Staggs continued matter-of-factly. "If I had a blood vessel that was bleeding and I needed to stop it very quickly before I could suture it, [I] would put a clamp on it to stop it." Then there are bandage scissors to cut bandages off. "This is specialized so you don't cut the patient. See how you have a blunt end?" she offered. Iris scissors, Mayo scissors, Metzenbaum scissors—there are thousands of different kinds of tools. Staggs described:

> These are Iris scissors. [They] are little delicate things. You're cutting delicate pieces of tissue. . . . So you might need to have

something that is at an angle. . . . Animals aren't straight and perpendicular, so you might just need to get around. . . . Mosquito hemostats are the [other] little ones. . . . These are retractors. When you open an animal up and you need to see, you could have somebody stand there, holding it open just with their hands. But instead . . . you put this in and then you press it and it opens to keep your surgical field open. So you can see down into the animal. . . . Then there are rongeurs . . . for snipping pieces of bone off. So in some of the fractures that we have, when you're putting them together, if there's a splintery end that just isn't coming together, you can just kind of trim it up and make it neat so it doesn't cause any more damage. Sometimes, there might be a defect in the bone so you need to clear it up. That's what we would use these for (interview).

My camera had a life of its own, and insisted on focusing on the veterinarian's hands, instead of on her face (see video presentation in Braverman 2020). The hands seemed to be doing their own thing, too, encompassing within their movement the secrets to a deeper understanding of the life of the mundane artifacts that the vet was telling me about.

Philosopher and retired medical physician and clinical neuroscientist Raymond Tallis was also fascinated with the human hand, suggesting that: "the hand inspired the tool-use that has come to dominate human life and which has led to the emergence of the complex symbolic systems—most importantly language—that underpin civilization" (2003). He argued, further, that:

> Herein lies the true genius of the hand: out of fractional finger movements comes an infinite variety of grips and their combinations. And from this variety in turn comes choice—not only what we do, but in how we do it. . . . With choice comes consciousness of acting: the arbitrariness of choice between two equally sensible ways of achieving the same goal awakens the sense of agency (2003, 174).

The realization of the importance of the hand for the use of tools invites further reflections on the particular nature of the tools used in animal procedures, as well as the continued co-production of agency through the interaction between human and animal bodies and tools. Despite the advancements in medical technology, simple daily tools remain crucial for medical procedures. Social studies of science scholars Christian Heath et al. reflected along these lines that:

> In recent years, we have witnessed a number of remarkable developments in surgical procedures and the technologies that are used to undertake operations. Notwithstanding these developments, many, if not most, procedures rely upon commonplace objects and artifacts—hammers, chisels, pliers, drills, scissors, tweezers and the like. . . . These implements and materials not only enable the performance of highly complex procedures but embody complex divisions of labour, knowledge and expertise that underpin their availability, deployment and use (2018).

Heath et al. call to take "the nonhuman, the material, and its agency seriously; to consider the interdependencies and interconnectedness of the human and nonhuman in action" (2018, see, e.g., Maller 2015). This and many other studies pertain to a human patient, and their encounter with the nonhuman is restricted mostly to things and artifacts. Engaging with the body of the nonhuman animal as a patient invites even further contemplations about networks across species divides.

Mundane Procedures

In December 2018, I traveled to the Shedd Aquarium in Chicago to shadow veterinarian Bill Van Bonn as he attended to the 32,000 animals in the aquarium. I was at that point hoping to witness a veterinary surgical procedure. It was one thing to write about them and see them in exhibits, and another to look into the insides of these animals, as I imagined my two days at Shedd to be. But a short time into my first interview with Van Bonn, I realized that my expectations from the visit may have been a tad too dramatic. "It isn't every day that we operate on a whale," he told me. In fact, he added, "I don't think we ever performed a major operation on a whale in this facility—and we hope to never have to do so." Instead, the vast majority of veterinary work involves observing and asking questions, conducting clinical pathology such as blood and urine tests, and using diagnostic imaging tools such as x-rays, ultrasounds, and endoscopies. "People want to jump to all kinds of exotic tools, including surgery," Van Bonn told me. But more often than not, "the most valuable thing to do is to ask questions and get the history."

Veterinarian Chris Dold of SeaWorld similarly emphasized the importance of the sensorial exam, using the term "organoleptic" to describe it. In his words,

> The first thing you're taught in most veterinary programs is how to do a visual and physical assessment of your patient before you should really allow yourself to do any laboratory testing, imaging, or any of those diagnostics. So use your senses before you use a tool. The word that sticks in my head that everyone here makes fun of me when I use it is *organoleptic*. Engage all of your senses for the purposes of diagnosis. So when I look at a group of dolphins like this [points to the dolphins we were observing, IB], my clinical mindset is always on (interview).

One of the most direct examples of sensing that I observed for this project occurred during a visit to Israel's only wildlife hospital, situated in Ramat Gan's Safari Zoological Center. During my visit, an ibex was brought in with severe wounds from dog bites (see Figure 3.9). The ibex was anesthetized and the wounds were

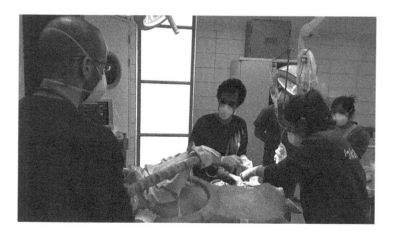

Figure 3.9 A Nubian ibex, suffering bite injuries after an attack by dogs in southern Israel, is operated on by a team of veterinarians led by veterinarian Yigal Horowitz at the Safari wildlife hospital in Ramat Gan, Israel. The ibex died a few days later. Photo by author, December 25, 2019.

cleaned and stitched. At that point, the two vets on the premise debated what to do with the black scab on one of the ibex's legs. The chief vet recommended doing nothing, as the animal was already compromised and needed some time to heal from the other wounds. The assistant vet disagreed. "Smell the leg," she insisted. "The flesh is rotten. We have to intervene at this point or the infection will spread." When he couldn't smell anything, everyone in the room was requested to pitch in on the quality of the smell. After an extended sniffing consortium, the majority agreed with the assistant, and so this exchange ended with an intervention on the other leg, too (Figure 3.10).

More generally, Van Bonn explained the typical development of an "animal case," and the importance of the physical exam in particular.

> VB: Getting the information can start with just asking questions, but very often you have to take the next step, which would be a physical exam. We use our senses—our hearing, our sight, our touch, our smell—not so much our taste but on occasion—to get additional information that we don't get from just speaking to the person [who] knows the animal the best.... A physical evaluation generally requires getting our hands on the animal, understanding the animal, feeling the

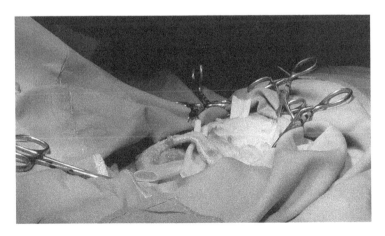

Figure 3.10 A bite injury to the Nubian ibex's hind leg. The wound was especially deep and required debridement and draining. Photo by author, December 25, 2019.

animal—is he soft or is he hard? If it's a puffer fish like the [one we saw together], his belly should be nice and soft; he should be squishy. If it felt like a hard baseball, that would raise concern because that would not be expected. . . .

IB: How would you know if you'd never touched a puffer fish?

VB: Well, we've touched lots of other types of fish [and], by nature, we're comparative.

IB: [Do] you have to touch a fish to know a fish?

VB: Yeah, absolutely. So, in that scenario I would say, "Okay, now I need even more information, just feeling it doesn't tell me what it is. How else can I learn what's causing the thing I'm feeling?" So then we [would typically] use tools to determine how well the animal is doing physiologically. . . . Next I would say "Let me see a blood sample or a urine sample." . . . Those windows into the health and welfare of the animal are incredibly powerful. With one sample of blood, I can tell you a lot about how the animal's liver is doing, how his kidney is doing, how his thyroid function is doing. . . . The next step is diagnostic imaging (interview).

Instead of the whale surgery I imagined for my Shedd Aquarium visit, I ended up attending a cross river puffer fish procedure. This 12-year-old fish was dealing with a skin issue. The cause of the wound was unclear, and Van Bonn had tried numerous treatments, including laser. The only treatment the fish responded to was Regranex Gel, an expensive topical ointment used for humans. Van Bonn elaborated:

The [fish's] skin wasn't growing back in, so what we have been doing is taking off the dead tissue around the edges and applying a substance called Regranex—and that helps it. [This is a] really unique medication. It is a human product—it's in fact a recombinant platelet-derived growth factor made specifically to stimulate epithelial growth for people who have chronic diabetes. Diabetes causes pathology to the very small vessels so these little small vessels become diseased, blood doesn't flow [and] doesn't bring the nutrients or oxygen to the tissues and they get all sorts of ulcers and problems. One of the things that doesn't get delivered there like it should is growth product for epithelia, so this product was designed for that. [This drug] is very expensive—it is not the standard thing you would [use]. The reason we're using it here is that we've tried all sorts of therapies on this guy that weren't successful, including laser therapy (interview).

As part of the procedure, the medium-sized cross river puffer fish needed to be anesthetized. For most of the time, the aquarist from the puffer's exhibit was the one who moved the fish from one tank to the next, using his bare hands (Van Bonn explained that fish "are not internally as sterile as we are" and have evolved to live with various critters. Even during surgery it is therefore not essential, and could in fact be counterproductive, "to be completely aseptic and wear a mask and glove and gown"). After some debate over quantity, the vet tech mixed a white anesthetic powder and poured it into the water. A few minutes later, the puffer fish was sedated enough that she (or he, the people in the room weren't quite sure, but the aquarist seemed to remember that her name was Pam) flipped over. That was the cue that it was time for the vet to take a look. Van Bonn asked another vet to manage the procedure as he didn't want to treat an animal while being distracted with an interview. When that veterinarian (whose name, incidentally, was also Pam) touched her, the affected area looked way too soft to me; it also seemed discolored, raw, and irritated. "This is great!" the two vets in the room exclaimed with much satisfaction. They weren't going to apply the gel after all, as the puffer fish seemed to be recovering on her own. They clearly had a completely different take than mine on the situation. Figures 3.11 and 3.12 are two of the many images that the Shedd Aquarium recorded to monitor the progress that Pam the puffer fish underwent, in light of which their satisfaction might make more sense.

The Clinical Outlook: Flipping the Lens

Chris Dold interned with the Marine Mammal Center and worked with the United States Navy Marine Mammal Program before he took the position of senior veterinarian at SeaWorld in 2005. He now serves as the Chief Zoological Officer there, overseeing all animal programs in the park, as well as rescue and rehabilitation, science, conservation, and education. As we walked through Sea-World together, I encouraged him to tell me how he sees the park's animals, and how his way of seeing differs from a laypersons' point of view. Here is a sliver of our conversation:

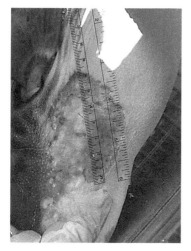 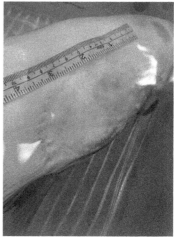

Figures 3.11 and 3.12 A cross river puffer fish before and after 13 treatments of unidentified skin problem with Regranex Gel, an expensive drug used for diabetic humans, conducted between March and December 2018. Courtesy of ©Shedd Aquarium.

IB: Is the capacity to see through a clinical eye something that can be turned on and off?

CD: For me, yes, absolutely. I see animals differently now, after I got my veterinary degree, than I did before, and I am not any less in awe of them. In fact, I'm more in awe. But there is definitely a switch you make through the veterinary education process. There is a kind of lens that I can flip down over my eyes and go into.

IB: Willingly?

CD: No, sometimes it's flipped for me and I can't necessarily predict it. I have three dogs, a cat, and an aquarium. We've got animals all over the house, and I don't go home going "How's everybody's health today?" But the first time I meet a dog I make a quick assessment. So it's like a shadow personality that's always there. It can creep up when you least expect it or when something new triggers it, like a model animal you've never seen before. I walk [through] the park [SeaWorld] as often as I possibly can. And when I do, I go into that clinical mode. [I practice] a herd health approach. If I were to care for cows I would do the same thing. I'd go through the whole herd and I'd say, "That one's skinny; that one's hiding in the corner; that one's ribs are showing." . . . You've got this list. And then you'll go individually and say, "Well, do any of the dolphins look particularly skinny? Do any of the dolphins look particularly overweight?" [But] I can still stand here and enjoy the dolphins having fun and playing. . .

IB: So the next obvious question is whether there is anything that this clinical mind is blind to?

CD: By definition, if you're blind to something, you're blind to it. So I don't necessarily know what we're blind to. Still, I would say that as a veterinarian, your proclivity is to minimize risks. The veterinarian's mindset is [that] nothing is fine until it is, and that's a bias, right? It's a bias. [By contrast,] as a daily caretaker or trainer or animal keeper your propensity is to assume that most things are fine.

Like Dold, many of the veterinarians I spoke with had mentioned the clinical lens, although often not by this name. Chris Walzer is the Executive Director of Health at the Wildlife Conservation Society in New York. During the past two decades, he has worked in the Gobi region of Mongolia, linking health with the conservation of the Asiatic wild ass (*Equus hemionus*). Here is how he described his own clinical lens:

> When I have a patient, it's a patient. I try to be concentrated: technically engaged, but emotionally distant. It's not that I don't care. I really care. But I understand that at that moment I need to really work. . . . I've done a lot of TV and films and people have pointed out to me [that] always when the procedure is over, I go up to the head of the animal and pat it or whisper something to it. [Once you] reverse the anesthesia you can sort of give a little bit of space to your emotions and say [to the animal], "Hey, have a good trip. Have a long and happy life," or whatever it is. Because you probably won't see that animal again. But while I'm working, that sounds gruesome, but I'm pretty cold in order to protect [myself if] it goes wrong. That's the other thing. . . . It's really rare that things go wrong, it's not like it happens all the time. But when it does, that little distance helps you. If you asked me and we sat down, I could

probably tell you each and every animal that I've lost. It's not many, but there are some where either I made a really bad decision, or I was tired, or it just went badly wrong for some reason. Sometimes it's beyond your control, but there are a few [times] where it was my mistake. I really wasn't being attentive (Walzer, interview).

The notion of caring while keeping an emotional distance is something that Science and Technology Studies scholar John Law reflects about in his study of veterinary work with British cattle. Similar to Walzer, Law suggests that care "is about responding, but not responding too much. It is about being there, about sensitivity, and yet it is also about distance. It is precisely about self-protection" (Law 2010, n.p.).

Whereas all experts put on a specialized lens, not all lenses are made of the same material. The veterinary lens is arguably unique not only for helping deal with the fleshiness of the body, but also for doing so in the context of nonhuman animals. Indeed, the veterinarians I encountered stressed how different their work is, on so many fronts, from that of medical doctors caring for humans. Specifically, while the zoo vets often pride themselves on the variety of animals they can and often do care for (Braverman 2018a), many of them emphasized that they "don't do humans." This might be a "lens" issue (namely, vets are not trained to put on the clinical lens in the context of humans), or it could be a practical and even a legal issue (related to liability, especially in the context of medical malpractice in the United States).

One way or the other, there seems to be a rigid divide between human and animal medical care. Under this divide, vets do not provide medical care for humans, although at times human physicians are invited to care for nonhuman animal patients. As mentioned in the Introduction, I was personally exposed to this rule during that unfortunate visit to the veterinary surgical room, where, overwhelmed by the fleshiness of the operated lizard, I found myself on the floor. I will quickly remind the reader that although the vet was aware that I had just fainted and suffered facial injuries, she continued to operate on the frilled-neck lizard without stopping to attend to her injured human guest. Whereas this behavior seemed odd at the time, inhumane even, a few other veterinarians explained to me later that this vet was simply following the rules—namely, veterinarians can only care for nonhuman animals, not for humans. Another vet told me along these lines that when, during a flight, the pilot asked whether there was a doctor onboard for an emergency, she did not respond.

Nili Avni-Magen from the Jerusalem Zoo was not as bifurcated in her approach toward human versus animal care. While she explained that most vets arrive at this profession because they *don't* want to be human doctors, she also emphasized that given a medical emergency, she would attend to the human in need. This has in fact happened to her when she was hiking with her family in a Jordanian desert, and a hiker emerged out of the blue to ask whether there was a doctor who could help with his friend's injury. She joined him and cared for his friend until a medical team (trained to care for humans) arrived.

The Art of Surgery: Peering into the Animal Body

> The ritual of surgery . . . is at once murderous, painful, healing, and full of love. Perhaps if one were to cut out a heart, a lobe of the liver, an entire convolution of the brain, and paste it to a page, it would speak with more eloquence than all the words of Balzac. Such a piece would need no literary style, no mass of erudition or history.
> —Richard Selzer, *The Art of Surgery*, 18

Although many of the zoo veterinarians I spoke with have become accustomed to behind-the-scenes work, often only visible to their institutional colleagues and to other veterinary practitioners, most of them were not opposed to, and were usually even interested in, exposing their work to the public eye. Two issues seem to prevent this from happening more frequently: the first is the routines that have been put in place with regard to invasive medical procedures, and the second is the wariness among zoo professionals about animal rights proponents who have categorically opposed zoos and who could make use of such footage against them. "For obvious reasons, we can't let you shoot any stills or videos behind the scenes," Shedd Aquarium's public relations officer instructed me mechanically. And although the reasons were far from obvious to me, I did not argue. I had already learned that one should always stay on the good side of public relations personnel, who are often the gatekeepers to all forms of communication with zoo and aquarium staff. Notably, the same public relations official was not at all bothered by my audio recordings. Control over the visual representations of their institutions seemed to be the main concern in this context.

Indeed, sight is powerful. And seeing such spaces that were previously invisible—doubly so. According to Van Bonn, the fleshiness of the nonhuman animal usually draws people in. "If they could, they would like to be completely inside the animal, see it as up-close as possible," he told me. In the marine center where he had previously worked, the necropsy room was designed with a window for public viewing. Van Bonn recalled that school children who stood outside would often bang on the window and demand to see things more closely. "Just give humans as much of this closeness to other creatures as possible," he commented warily. Philosopher Mary Midgley's realizations in *Beast and Man* are important in this context. She writes: "We are not just rather like animals; we are animals. Our difference from other species may be striking, but comparisons with them have always been, and must be, crucial to our view of ourselves" (2005, n.p.). The fascination with flesh, ours and theirs, can be understood as a fascination with the foundations of these similarities—and differences.

Yet, alongside the fascination with flesh—and especially with the fleshiness of the other-than-us who is at the same time also so very similar-to-us—there is also a sense that fleshy matters and imageries can be appalling, gory, and repulsive to many. Others are uncomfortable with what they perceive as the pornographic dimension of this spectacle. Recall in this context the upset that the dissection of Marius the giraffe triggered around the world. Similarly, warnings about "graphic content" often accompany relevant video presentations of zoo vet surgeries and procedures released to the public. Along these lines, the publisher of this book has advised me to pull out certain images that readers might not expect to encounter in a non-medical book and to also add words of caution in the Introduction about the remaining images.

How do veterinarians feel about the fleshy aspects of their work? Whereas Van Bonn attested that he has no qualms about such procedures, other medical practitioners may feel differently, as can be gleaned from surgeon Richard Selzer's *The Art of Surgery* (which focuses on human bodies):

Even now, after so many voyages within, so much exploration, I feel the same sense that one should not gaze into the body, the same irrational fear that it is an evil deed for which punishment awaits. Consider. The sight of our internal organs is denied us. To how many men is it given to look upon their own spleens, their hearts, and live? ([1974] 1996, 24).

Arguably, the most radical expression of the clinical lens in the surgical procedure, when the human eye peers into the body of the other (see, e.g., Figure 3.13). Melissa Joblon, assistant veterinarian at the New England Aquarium, explained that she never had an issue with such peering, even in her early days as a lab technician studying the brain of apes. That is, until she herself was charged with responsibility for the process. In her words:

> I never had that weird, queasy feeling [that other vets sometimes talk about]. It's something that had never bothered me. [But] I found it completely different when I became the primary person doing it. So when I was an assistant, I was perfectly

Figure 3.13 A stingray surgery at the Denmark National Aquarium, Den Blå Planet. Photo by Anders Engrob. Courtesy of Kasper Jørgensen.

calm, cool, and collected. But when I first started doing surgeries on my own as a doctor, I remember getting, never queasy, but that nervous feeling because it's me in charge. I remember the initial soft tissue handling. It was honestly a little bit terrifying because when something starts to bleed, you're always used, as an assistant, to just sit there and dab. The doctor will do what is needed. Now, it's me who has to figure out where it's bleeding. So, it's a completely different world, where your mind has to be in a completely different place. But you get used to it and it's all about experience. I'm still learning surgery. But I love it now. Now, it's exciting, it's fun (Joblon, interview).

Conclusion

Dolphins and whales are magical. But then so are dogs. And bacteria. If you simply stop to take a look at these things— holy cow!

—Bill Van Bonn, interview

This chapter has provided a glimpse into the material and technological aspects of the zoo veterinarian's work, aiming to expose readers from the social sciences and humanities to the lifeworld of zoo and aquarium veterinarians and to their ecology of practice. Specifically, I examined the vets' clinical perspectives on what it means to care closely for animals in a captive setting. And although theirs is admittedly not the only perspective available on how to care for these animals, it is nonetheless a valuable one. To understand it, we must make an effort to immerse ourselves in the vets' professional world and to familiarize ourselves with their tools and techniques, with their routines and ways of knowing. This includes quite a bit of attendance to flesh and tools—to hands, scissors, machines, ointments, needles, medicines, and even guns.

Beyond their mastery in "hands-on" care for the bodies of their individual animals, over the last decade or so the work of the zoo veterinarian has also expanded to encompass the "body multiple" (Mol 2002) of individual, population, and ecosystem health. In this One Health context, practicing veterinary medicine is less about scissor skills, and more about integrating monitoring techniques and quantitative modeling approaches that offer opportunities to combine data from veterinary medicine with ecological concepts and with mathematical epidemiology (Walzer 2017, 3). Unlike conditions at the zoo, *in situ* conditions require the adjustment of laboratory practices and the development of novel technologies such as portable real-time polymerase chain reaction (PCR), genome sequencing, eDNA sampling for pathogens, and a multitude of functional immunological tests that further facilitate integration across disciplines (Walzer 2017; see also Marx 2015, 396). Even when there are no classic lab benches or electrical outlets, PCR samples can be tested on portable devices, allowing veterinarians to "hunt for pathogens" that affect dynamic ecosystems in a timely manner. As one conservation medicine proponent put it: "We have to bridge the gap between the people in muddy boots and jeans and those in white coats" (Pokras, quoted in Norris 2001, 10).

More than a fashion statement, bridging the gap between muddy jeans and white coats speaks to the novel identity of the zoo veterinarian, who brings into the conversation "the broadest multidisciplinary sense along a gradient from captive to free-ranging wildlife and across all taxa" as relating to the "human-domestic pet-livestock-wildlife interface" (Walzer 2017, 3). Due to their multiple existence in such interface spaces, zoo veterinarians are well-positioned to undertake the complex project of caring for the earth's diverse life forms. The scope of the new zoo veterinarian's expertise, then, "includes not only the core fields of veterinary medicine such as surgery, anesthesia, physiology, pathology, immunology, anatomy, epidemiology, and animal welfare as they relate to wildlife but also incorporates fields including but not limited to ecology, conservation biology, economics, and the social sciences" (2017, 3).

This was but a quick taste of the fleshy aspects of vet medicine—and that which lies beyond the flesh. Much more work on veterinary anthropology still awaits. And with it, an opportunity to bridge the much-too-dangerous, and widening, gap between the hard and soft sciences, and between humans and others. Circling back to Stengers, I would offer that we ought to "meddle in what is meant not to concern us" (2000, 46). Not doing so would be granting too much power to the experts who manage these spaces and interactions. At this very particular juncture, meddling is not a choice but a responsibility: we must collaborate to break the divisive silos that have come to characterize our universities, disciplines, and lives.

Chapter 4

Caring and Killing
Euthanasia in Zoos and Aquariums

> This is not what I trained for.
> I hope familiarity will never make me immune from the trauma of killing.
> But I do hope—for the animal's sake—to be good at it.
> —Frost-Pennington 2001, 8 (quoted in Law 2010, n.p.)

Killing Animals: An Introduction

One of the central questions in animal care, in zoos and elsewhere, is when, where, and how much should humans intervene in animal life. The most dramatic site of such interventions, and, possibly, also the most frequent one (Haraway 2008), is the act of killing nonhuman animals. Belgian philosopher of science Vinciane Despret notes that: "Those who might doubt this have probably forgotten all of the massacres of the last few years, whether due to mad cow disease, avian influenza, foot and mouth disease, or scrapie" (2016, 83). According to Science and Technology Studies and feminist scholar Donna Haraway: "there is no way of living that is not also a way of someone, not just something, else dying differentially" (2008, 80).

A variety of practices account for the killing of animals by humans—from the hunting of wild animals, through the slaughter of farm animals, to the killing of dangerous animals and the culling of pests, all the way to acts of killing for cruelty or amusement. Each one of these practices engages its own methods, which are aligned with its purposes, and also receives a different term. As animal geographer Chris Wilbert writes in the introduction to his edited collection *Killing Animals*: "Indeed, the extent and the variety of the killing is reflected in the number of terms we use to describe these different types of death. Animals become extinct. They are also killed, gassed, electrocuted, exterminated, hunted, butchered, vivisected, shot, trapped, snared, run over, lethally injected, culled, sacrificed, slaughtered, executed, euthanized, destroyed, put down, put to sleep, and even, perhaps, murdered" (2006, 5–6).

Wilbert also points out that the deliberate killing of animals, at least in most industrialized nations, is largely invisible in the public domain. Some of the zoo veterinarians I interviewed were indeed not always keen to speak with me about this aspect of their work, not only for the sensitivity of the topic but also because they often perceived it as a tactic used by animal rights groups to undermine the zoos' very existence. The tensions between animal rights activists and zoo advocates received a dramatic exposure when Marius the giraffe was euthanized, culled, killed, or murdered—the precise terminology dependent on who you speak with about the event.

The form of killing that this chapter is concerned with is euthanasia, a term derived from the Greek *eu* (good) and *thanatos* (death). According to the AVMA Guidelines, a "good death" is one that occurs with minimal pain and distress to the animal (AVMA 2013). In this way of thinking, animal suffering is negative and, taken to its extreme, is unacceptable and should be avoided. This approach has resulted in what some have called a "culture of euthanasia," whereby euthanasia is perceived by many Western veterinarians not only as morally laudable but also as legally mandated in certain situations.

Strikingly at odds with the way we consider the suffering and death of humans, veterinarians seem to think that, for animals, suffering is worse than death, which, in itself, is not perceived as a harm (McMahan 2002; Pierce 2016). But what *is* suffering? A group of vets responded: "Suffering is an unpleasant state of mind that disrupts the quality of life. It is the mental state associated with unpleasant experiences such as pain, malaise, distress, injury and emotional numbness. . . . [P]ain, probably more than any other state, directly reduces welfare" (Föllmi et al. 2007, 309, 313). A survey of 41 veterinary surgeons found that 86 percent felt that euthanasia was a necessary and important part of their professional role (cited in Hurn and Badman-King 2019, 144). In addition to its occurrence in veterinary clinics and shelters (Abrell 2016; Pierce 2016), euthanasia also takes place in rescue and rehabilitation centers (Karesh 1995; Moore et al. 2014; Palmer 2018), in the wild, and in zoos and aquariums. This chapter focuses on the euthanasia of wild animals performed by zoo veterinarians in zoos and aquariums as well as in rescue centers and *in situ* settings.

Generally, zoo animals are considered the property of their human owners and are thus governed by the welfare-oriented rules and standards that pertain to this form of property. But accredited zoo guidelines around the globe have expanded euthanasia beyond its traditional welfare aims, using it as a tool for the management of zoo populations. In 2011, the European Association of Zoos and Aquariums (EAZA) issued a Euthanasia Statement that articulated four instances in which euthanasia should be considered. Here, word-for-word:

1. Where the animal poses a serious and unavoidable threat to human safety, e.g. escaped animals.
2. Where, in the opinion of the staff responsible for the individual animal's health and welfare, an animal is suffering from a disease, detrimental psychological state or severe pain and stress which cannot be adequately alleviated.
3. Where the only alternative is permanent transfer to substandard accommodation.
4. Where the continued presence of an individual animal is disruptive to the natural dynamic of a group within an individual collection and/or the demographic or genetic health and development of an EAZA approved *ex-situ* conservation programme. Consequently, young animals (e.g. at weaning or when normally leaving parental care) and animals that are past breeding age or are senile (groups that are prone to deleterious geriatric conditions) may be considered for euthanasia as part of a balanced population management strategy (EAZA Euthanasia Statement 2011).

Clearly, then, long before Marius was killed, accredited zoos in Europe were already fully on board with what they defined as different types of euthanasia, in addition to the medical-based euthanasia articulated in Article 2 of the Statement. Specifically, Article 4 provides detailed examples for when animals should be killed "as part of a balanced population management strategy."

Similar guidelines have been issued by accreditation institutions around the world. For example, the Australasia zoo guidelines state that: "[e]uthanasia is considered a necessary procedure that supports sound animal welfare outcomes in the responsible application of veterinary medicine and in some circumstances as part of the scientific management of animal populations" (ZAAA 2015). The South East Asian Zoo Association (SEAZA) was more reserved about such practices when articulating in its Constitution that: "Euthanasia may be controlled by local customs and laws but should always be used in preference to keeping an animal alive under conditions which do not allow it to experience an appropriate quality of life" (SEAZA n.d., Article V).

While medical euthanasia is widely accepted in accredited zoos and aquariums in developed countries, the killing of healthy animals for conservation and management purposes has been quite controversial. The strong emotional reactions to the killing of Marius the giraffe by the Copenhagen Zoo shed light onto this largely invisible practice, which some approve of and refer to as "culling," while others condemn it. Ecologist Marc Bekoff, an outspoken critic of this practice, has dubbed it "zoothanasia." In his words: "Killing animals in zoos because they don't 'figure into breeding plans' is not euthanasia, it's 'zoothanasia,' and is a most disturbing and inhumane practice" (Bekoff 2012). Debates outside of the zoo community aside, the killing of Marius has also exposed the disagreements among zoos and aquariums about whether, and how much, euthanasia ought to be utilized within their facilities and, if so, how exactly it should be performed—for example, by gun or injection, with public necropsy or behind closed doors, with feeding the flesh to other animals or not, and so forth.

Euthanasia in Humans versus Nonhumans

Although euthanasia can refer to ending the life of both human and nonhuman animals, what qualifies as euthanasia for each group differs considerably. As Patricia Morris explains in her book *Blue Juice: Euthanasia in Veterinary Medicine*: "For humans, calling a death euthanasia is restricted to circumstances of mercy killing, in which death is a welcome relief from prolonged pain and suffering. For nonhuman animals, a good death is defined not by motive but by method. In other words, so long as death is without pain and distress, animals are *euthanized* in animal shelters, veterinary offices, and research laboratories for the convenience and benefit of humans" (Morris 2012, 8; emphasis in original).

In the human context, euthanasia is quite controversial and has resulted in a complex regulatory matrix that includes distinctions between active and passive euthanasia, as well as the category of "assisted killing" by medical professionals. Whereas active euthanasia is illegal throughout the United States, except for Oregon, human patients may retain the right to refuse treatment, what is referred to as passive euthanasia. By contrast, tens of thousands of animals are euthanized *every day* in the United States alone. Such animal killing takes place not only in the offices of veterinarians but also in animal shelters, where millions of dogs and cats are euthanized each year by non-vets (Alper 2008, 837). As Jessica Pierce put it: "Euthanasia is part of the well-greased machinery of the pet industry. . . . Every eleven seconds, a healthy dog or cat is euthanized in U.S. shelters. The pet consumer is convinced that this euthanasia—we mustn't call it killing—is necessary, and is, furthermore, an act of compassion" (2016, 136).

Despite the bitter disputes between them, the veterinary and animal welfare communities are in fact in full agreement about the safest and most humane method of animal euthanasia: an anesthetic-only procedure involving an overdose of sodium pentobarbital. This method has been utilized in the United States for more than 60 years (Alper 2008). The veterinary and animal welfare communities also condemn the use of neuromuscular blocking agents that first cause paralysis. Yet despite this broad condemnation, this method has been used for humans on death row. Ty Alper notes that "the use of such drugs in animal euthanasia is actually *illegal* in many states that nevertheless continue to use them in human lethal injections" (2008, 839; emphasis in original). In his view, this strange disparity is largely due to the misconception that it would seem inhumane to kill humans in the same way that one would kill nonhuman animals (Alper 2008, 817). As in many instances explored in this book, here, too, the insistence on maintaining rigid human–animal distinctions results in ethically problematic—and painful—consequences.

Euthanasia of Zoo Animals for Medical Reasons

The veterinarians I spoke with distinguish between two general types of euthanasia: medical euthanasia and the killing of healthy animals for managerial purposes. There is a stark divide on this front between northern European zoos and the major accredited zoos in the United States, chief veterinarian at the Jerusalem Zoo

Nili Avni-Magen told me in our interview. Certain North European zoos not only euthanize for a variety of reasons beyond the medical ones, she explained, but they will also often opt to euthanize more frequently within the scope of medical reasons if there are sustainability concerns or for conservation purposes. By contrast, American zoos tend to use physical separation and contraception to avoid the reproduction of "surplus" animals, thereby minimizing the need to euthanize these animals later. This form of preventative management at the same time limits the zoo animals' ability to practice reproductive and other natural behaviors (Braverman 2012, 174–180).

With the heightened level of medical care in zoos and the lack of predators there, zoo animals often live longer than their wild counterparts (Vogelnest and Talbot 2019, 83). Because of their reluctance to euthanize, North American zoo vets will often attempt to accommodate these geriatric and compromised animals, in some cases providing them with highly expensive cancer and heart treatments. By contrast, other zoos—vocally represented by northern European institutions—hold that such treatments would condemn their animals to painful lives, while the already well-represented animal also occupies a much-needed space without making a significant contribution to the zoos' collaborative breeding programs (Föllmi et al. 2007, 309). According to this latter approach, "a good zoo strives to improve the quality of its animals' lives, not necessarily their length of life" (Föllmi et al. 2007, 313; see also Vogelnest and Talbot 2019, 83).

The extent to which euthanasia is undesirable in the United States, even in medical instances and with geriatric animals who do not directly contribute to the population, was on clear display during my visit with veterinarian Lydia Staggs at SeaWorld, in which she introduced me to a 12-year-old otter with breast cancer. Here is a sliver of the conversation that ensued:

> LS: We did what is called a radical bilateral mastectomy, where I removed not only the breast tissue but the lymph nodes. When that occurred, we took her to a hospital and had a CT scan for her lungs on her. We saw that a little metastasis had already started in her chest. And so we contacted a veterinary oncologist who was very willing to help. . . . We did research, we contacted other zoos and aquariums. This was a rare thing to see. Pulling from other species and other treatments, the

oncologist and I came up with a chemotherapy protocol that was safe for her. She seems to be doing well with it.
IB: How long has she been on it?
LS: Six months now.
IB: How long is it supposed to continue?
LS: Well, she will probably always be on the chemotherapy drug, at least one of them, for the rest of her life.
IB: That is probably not cheap.
LS: No, it's not. But we do it because it's the right thing to do. It's our responsibility. We made a pledge and have a responsibility to take care of these animals for their entire lives. She was a "show" otter. She's retired now. But again, it's the right pledge. You take care of animals the whole length of the time that they're with us. And as for costs, I don't really know [and don't concern myself with this issue]. [As our Park's President always says:] you worry about the animals—and we will worry about the money.

Although SeaWorld's particular history could perhaps cast a shadow on the attempts to save this otter (after all, when Blackfish came out and exposed SeaWorld's dealings with orcas, this commercial institution faced an economic crisis; and they are still exhibiting orcas—see, e.g., Figure 4.1), I'd like to suggest that the supreme treatment offered to the otter, taken to the extreme here, is also representative of a broader tendency among North American accredited zoos toward radical expressions of welfare—for certain animals at least. It also exemplifies the role of the zoo as a lab, and of the zoo animal as an experimental subject in the hands of the zoo vet, thereby signifying this profession's shift from being purely welfare-oriented to one that focuses on generating medical knowledge about wild animals at large.

When I relayed the details of my visit at SeaWorld and the extensive cancer treatments of their geriatric otter to Copenhagen Zoo's veterinarian Mads Bertelsen (the vet who killed Marius), he was baffled. "I just can't understand it," he said. "This would never happen here. If there is any doubt that a geriatric animal might be suffering, then there's no doubt that it has to go" (interview). It is not that he looks for opportunities to kill, Bertselsen explained, but since zoos are in dire need for space, killing this otter and others in her situation "would leave space and resources for animals that are valuable to the real goals that we're trying to

Figure 4.1 Veterinarian Lydia Staggs performs a routine ultrasound on an orca at SeaWorld, Florida. Photo by author, September 27, 2019.

advance: actually saving species." Bertelsen then went on to reflect on an e-mail post on the global zoo veterinarian listserv that he happened to read that same morning, in which a highly respected American veterinarian asked for advice regarding a sick capybara. Bertelsen commented:

> That doesn't make any sense. We have 10 capybaras here and we're probably going to euthanize 8 of them. So I almost wrote him an e-mail [response] to say, "Well, how many of them do you want?!" . . . He's putting all those resources into harassing that animal [supposedly] to save his life. But the animal doesn't know that. So it's just going to experience numerous surgeries and pain. Why [is he] doing that? If he's not doing that for the animal, he's doing that for himself or he's doing that for the zoo. [In any case, he's doing it] for the wrong reasons.

Bertelsen's view on this topic is uncompromising. For him, this approach clearly "originates from the whole Disney fixation, where it's suddenly 'Molly the capybara' and 'Molly deserves the very best.' And it's done because the keepers like it [and] the public loves it. For a veterinarian, it can be very satisfying, too, [to] 'save' that animal. But to what end?" Bertelsen especially takes issue with the widely pronounced argument that zoo veterinarians should not play God by killing animals. In his words:

> We made that decision when we brought these animals into our care. [From that point on,] I play God every single day. When I put an animal into an enclosure, I decide when it eats, what it needs, who it spends its time with, when the light turns out, when the rain comes—I decide everything. And, of course, I also decide when it lives and when it dies.

In their role as the gods of zoo animals, zoo veterinarians must operate based on ecological goals, in Bertelsen's view. Committed first and foremost to saving species in the wild, "zoos have to make up their mind if they want the popularity vote for saving Molly the capybara, or they want to be relevant on the bigger scale for conservation. It's difficult to do both at the same time, not to say impossible."

Many zoo veterinarians I spoke with adamantly disagreed with Bertelsen's approach. The chief veterinarian of Israel's Ramat Gan Safari Zoological Center, Yigal Horowitz, had this to say about veterinarians adopting ecological goals (and "going wild," as I called it earlier):

> I am not an ecologist, I am a veterinarian. I chose this profession precisely because I wanted to care for animals. If I were an ecologist, I might ask myself other questions. If a murderer arrives at the hospital, it isn't up to the physician to decide if to care for him or not. He takes care of him, and then the legal system will judge if he had committed murder and whether he should die for that. In the same manner, I don't ask myself these questions. I think as a veterinarian. If one wants to adopt an ecological approach, let him be an ecologist (Horowitz, interview).

The same veterinarian also described how he put his job on the line to protect his independence with regard to euthanasia decisions. In his words:

> The [Safari's] director called me in. He wanted to assemble a committee with a zoologist, the keeper, as well as myself

and him, where each of us would say what we think needs to happen with the animal and then we would all decide together [about euthanizing that animal.] "So who would implement the decision?" I asked, to which the director replied, "You, of course." "But what if I don't agree that this animal needs to be euthanized, do I still need to execute this decision?" I insisted, and he confirmed. I refused right then and there. I told him that ten committees can tell me to kill an animal, but if it's against my best judgement, I will never do it. I also told him that he is welcome to fire me, I am not anyone's executioner. There was a lot of screaming and yelling in front of everyone, but I didn't budge (Horowitz, interview).

Horowitz's insistence that any decision to euthanize an animal can only be based on his own professional judgement stands out in the zoo's culture of collective decision-making processes about husbandry, breeding, reintroductions, and everything else in between. For him, the decision to kill is unique and distinct from all other decisions made by the zoo veterinarian. Conversely, for Jerusalem Zoo's chief veterinarian Nili Avni-Magen, a decision about euthanasia is one that *must* be made collectively by her zoo's entire committee. There are different institutional cultures with respect to euthanasia, she explained. At her zoo, she would never kill an animal unless the keeper was on board. The decision to do so would involve an open conversation between several zoo staff—the keeper, the curator, the director, and her—who would each bring a different perspective to the table. Bertelsen clarified in this context that while euthanasia is a relatively easy procedure, it is the decision to do it that is often difficult. In his words, "if you anesthetize an animal, which we do many times a day, then the next step, if it's euthanasia, is just to give it an overdose. Technically, it's a very easy task. The difficulty lies in making sure that it's the right thing to do."

One of the veterinarians I interviewed, who preferred to remain anonymous, emphasized that the individual welfare ethic that has informed modern veterinary school has resulted in substantially different approaches between the older and younger generations of veterinarians. These are especially pronounced in the context of euthanasia. In his words:

> People sometimes want [to become vets] because they love animals. They cannot see a dog or a cat suffering, so they go to vet

school to prevent that. What I usually say to these people [is]: Don't go to vet school, because you won't be able to deal with some of the issues that a vet should deal with. For example: slaughter. Have you ever been to a slaughter house? This is very hard. But veterinary work started like that—vets started as inspectors of meat. Nowadays, you have veterinary students who say "I will not go inside that slaughter house." [But] how can you be a vet if you don't go in there? This is a reflection that you are not able to face current day problems and complexities. I can't say "I will not do euthanasia." Well, it's very easy to say it, but then who will suffer more? The animal, not me! And the big problem is that, with time, the mentality of the veterinarian profession is changing. And this is not good [for the animals].

As this veterinarian pointed out, zoo and aquarium veterinarians must often decide upon, perform, and deal with the consequences of the very real death of the animals under their care. For this reason, he is concerned that animal rights sentiments may hinder veterinary work, and especially so when conservation purposes dictate non-medical euthanasia. Similarly, Chris Walzer of the Wildlife Conservation Society shared in our interview that students come to his conservation medicine classes only in their last year of vet school, after spending their earlier studies and training dealing with individual dogs, cats, and horses. "So it's very hard for them to switch and say, 'Look, unfortunately we need to kill this animal.'" Avni-Magen recounted along these lines that "as a young zoo vet I was delighted to see a dog in a wheelchair." Nowadays, however, she sees things differently. She went on to explain:

> Instead of extending its suffering, I now realize what a real privilege it is that I can offer euthanasia to a suffering animal. I have come to see the animal and its meaning as part of a larger population and network. At the same time, I [must admit that] have a hard time letting go of my fallow deer as part of their reintroduction into the wild, when I know that some 40 percent of these animals will die in the [release] process and that they would much rather stay here at the zoo (Avni-Magen, interview).

When killing for medical reasons, the question is not *if* but *when* to euthanize. In other words: when is an animal's pain so immense that it justifies intervention in her life course? Hence, even in the case of the geriatric otter from SeaWorld, Staggs was clear about her responsibility to kill this animal at a later point. With this in mind, she explained the difference between caring for human and nonhuman animals, and the importance of euthanasia for the latter. In her words:

> We don't treat [animals] like [we treat] humans. We aren't trying to necessarily get rid of the cancer. We want to treat to make sure the animal feels better. And so, if we can cause the disease to go into remission, great, but we're not going to have them vomiting and being sick and losing all their fur. We don't do that to them. So it's a different approach than what we take with human beings. Because, again, you can explain to your human being: "This is our goal, We're trying to treat this to get you here, to extend your life." You can't explain that to an otter. They know: "I don't feel well. I don't want to eat." It's a totally different mindset, [which results in] a totally different [medical] approach (Staggs, interview).

For euthanasia to be the last resort, Staggs put enormous efforts into extending the life of the 12-year old otter, who is what Sea-World refers to as a "show animal" (in other words, she was not part of a sustainable zoo population in the first place). By contrast, in the eyes of many other zoo veterinarians, this particular otter's life would be considered meaningless. Swiss veterinarian Jérôme Föllmi argues, for instance, that euthanasia is often problematically delayed by zoos to the detriment of the animal's welfare. Based on a study of 70 geriatric zoo mammals in five European zoos, he established a scoring system for geriatric zoo mammals dedicated to "establish[ing] an initial objective decision making framework for the euthanasia of geriatric zoo mammals" (Föllmi et al. 2007, 309).

Similarly, Vogelnest and Talbot have called to "develop a methodology and database to identify animals approaching or beyond an average or 'expected longevity' for the species," suggesting that when a zoo animal reaches 80 percent of expected longevity for the species, an assessment process should commence that includes physical examination as well as the application of welfare assessment tools like Chicago Zoological Society's WelfareTrak® (2019, 90). Zoo veterinarians in Western accredited facilities utilize such standards, and others like them, in cases where the condition of the animal is not obvious (for example, Vogelnest told me in our interview that he uses a 20 percent total body surface assessment, which is imported from human medicine, to decide if wild animals should be euthanized for burns). However, when the animal is clearly suffering, or if a surgery is the last ditch effort to save her (such as in the case of the lizard I described in the Introduction), the decision is straightforward and does not require the utilization of scoring systems (Bertelsen & Avni-Magen, interviews).

Another point of contention is *how* best to euthanize. According to Bertelsen, a shot in the head would be the most efficient and pain-free method in many instances. In his words: "whereas a rifle bullet to the brain sounds dramatic, it is actually the only way that we can do it completely stress-free." This method has the additional benefit that the flesh of the killed animal could later be fed to other zoo animals (when using anesthesia, the drug spreads through the body and renders it inedible). But staff and visitors often respond badly to the bullet-in-the-head method, Bertelsen said, explaining that "it's noisy, there's lots of blood and the animal typically would have some kind of cramps or tremors after it's actually dead." "While it looks bad," he continued, "it isn't *actually* bad. [Still,] anesthesia and an overdose is much more controlled, and is quiet. So unless we need to feed the animals, that's typically what we go for."

Another group of animals who are killed in the zoo context, but who are often left out of the discussion on euthanasia, are domestic or farm animals who are used as food for the meat-eating zoo animals. While such animal deaths usually occur outside of the zoo space, some zoo veterinarians are nonetheless concerned about how these animals have died. Veterinarian Iman Memarian, formerly of the Tehran Zoo, shared in this context that in Iran, such food animals are killed using the same method used for animals designated for human consumption, thus abiding by Sharia law, which is not always animal welfare friendly. In his words: "They cut the head. But since it is impossible to cut the head off completely, the spinal cord is still attached, and so the animal can feel the pain. I have advised them to use a lighter drug inside the spinal cord so the animal cannot feel it." According to Memarian, domestic animals used as food for zoo animals should be euthanized, rather than slaughtered. All this would require is a slight shift in awareness, he said, which would in turn make a big difference for the welfare of numerous animals. At the same time, Memarian also emphasized that euthanasia for welfare purposes is only one half of his ethic as a veterinarian. The other half is his commitment to wildlife conservation. He has two rules for euthanasia, he told me. "The first is [to kill] when I think that if I keep this animal alive, it will suffer, and the second is [to kill] when I think that an animal would be really dangerous for wildlife conservation" (interview). Memarian elaborated that he would euthanize injured animals who reached the zoo or the rehabilitation center (where he also worked) if they were members of an "invasive" species. The extension of euthanasia to encompass such invasive wild animals beyond the confines of the zoo signals a move away from the zoo veterinarian's traditional role into new domains as an agent of conservation. Notably, this type of euthanasia of wild members of invasive species is still a contentious practice among vets.

Euthanasia is not very popular in Iran—neither for humans nor for pets, and not even for wild or zoo animals. "You are not God to decide on these things," Memarian explained how his fellow countrymen react to this practice. "In Iran, the problem is magic," he continued. "Everybody believes in magic." But as veterinarians, he said, we do not believe in magic. "We cannot wait for God to say *toop* and the animal would be walking again. If you keep this animal in that situation, it will suffer and you will be responsible for this suffering if you don't perform euthanasia." I can give you an example, he offered, and proceeded to relay a story about his encounter with the largest leopard in the world, which sounded like it was pulled straight out of the Arabian Nights:

> We found the Persian leopard with one limb amputated. But this animal was able to hunt for more than two months at least because the wound was totally cured. Then, we found the animal in a situation in which both hind limbs were totally paralyzed. [When] we anesthetized it, we found around 60 bullets inside its body. With one hand amputated, it was not possible for this animal to hunt in the wild. So it came to the village and fed on the domestic animals. Most of the farmers tried to shoot the animal. At last, one of the bullets went through the spinal canal and the animal was completely paralyzed. This leopard was the biggest leopard ever recorded anywhere in the

Figure 4.2 Using T-61, veterinarian Iman Memerian euthanized the largest Persian leopard ever recorded, weighing 110 kg, in Iran, 2008. Photo credit: Alireza Shahrdaripanah.

world. After we did radiographs and a CT scan on the spinal cord, we confirmed that we cannot do anything for it. [At this point], the animal started eating his own hind limbs, [probably] because he thought that they were not really useful. It was a really bad situation. So we decided to euthanize the animal. It was really a necessity to do that [since] we do not believe in magic (see Figure 4.2).

The Western veterinarians I interviewed would likely all agree that this leopard presents an easy case for medical euthanasia. Because they do not believe in "magic" or in divine interventions, it becomes the responsibility of the scientifically educated veterinarian to end animal suffering in the least painful way possible. Killing, in other words, is perceived by vets as the ultimate form of caring in this context (for a discussion of the parallel killing–caring duality in the lab, see Arluke 1988; Holmberg 2011).

An important aspect of the Iranian leopard story is that the animal euthanized by the zoo veterinarian was a wild-caught leopard, not a zoo animal. But before I move to discuss euthanasia of non-zoo animals, a quick note of qualification regarding the discussion's geographic and cultural specificity. Admittedly, this book has focused on zoos from developed countries, and so the norms pertaining to euthanasia are discussed from that perspective, too. By contrast, Vogelnest of the Taronga Zoo, who spent time working in Southeast Asia, noted that zoo veterinarians in East and South Asia typically do not adhere to the Western medical euthanasia standards with regard to geriatric animals. "I've worked in Vietnam and China," he told me, "and the vets there are very different." One of the examples he provided was from the time he was shown around a zoo in China and saw an "ancient tiger" living in a small cage in the back. "It so clearly needed to be euthanized," he recounted. "But the zoo's vet wasn't even talking about it" (interview).

Euthanasia of Non-Zoo Wild Animals

In addition to conducting medical-based euthanasia on zoo animals within the confines of zoos and aquariums, zoo veterinarians also increasingly euthanize wild animals who are imperiled *in situ*, or who are brought to the zoo by the public. I happened to witness such an occurrence during my visit to SeaWorld, when the aquarium's rescue team responded to a call from local residents who reported an injured sandhill crane (*Grus canadensis*). The crane had fractured his leg and seemed quite compromised, so Staggs performed a quick physical exam. While no one spoke explicitly about euthanasia, the mood in the room had shifted abruptly after the exam. As the team was preparing for the euthanasia procedure, I asked Staggs why such a seemingly confined fracture necessitated it. This is the conversation that ensued:

> LS: Remember, he's a wild bird. He'd have to be in a sling to support him. And based on our experience, they don't do well with that. So we [might] think, "Oh, it's just a broken leg." But in this case it's . . .
> IB: Death in the wild, basically?
> LS: Right. We've tried pinning legs and we've tried pinning other fractures. They just don't do well, they don't recover. They'll get bumble foot, which is an infection on the weight bearing foot. And chances are that the infection will set into this bone. And [so we euthanize] to prevent that suffering.

IB: Hmm. Could you give him more anesthesia? And how do you know how much is enough?
LS: It is going to go under anesthesia, and then we will go get the euthanasia solution, which is what you use in dog and cat medicine to euthanize an animal, and we will inject that intravenously into the animal. It'll stop its heart and it's very peaceful.
IB: How long does it take?
LS: Seconds. . . . We want to make sure they're under anesthesia before we do it.
IB: How often does this happen?
LS: More than we would like. It happens probably several times a week.

During the euthanasia procedure, the staff fell silent, and it became quite clear that continuing to shoot my video was inappropriate. Staggs promptly reflected that, "Every animal is given the same level of respect when we do this. You notice [that] there is no music playing and it's very quiet. It's a very serious thing to take a life." The procedure was performed in complete silence from start to finish. Although I was not exposed to the sight of blood or to any other gory details, I felt like the world around me was spinning and decided that it might be advisable, this time, to ask for a chair. And there I sat, while every other human in the room was standing, until this crane's life was over in a matter of minutes.

Experiencing the routinized practice of euthanasia firsthand reminded me of the question asked by feminist philosopher Judith Butler: "Whose lives count as lives?", which she related to the more concrete question: "What makes for a grievable life?" (Butler 2004, 26). Cary Wolfe extended these questions, which Butler asked about humans, also to animals (2012, 18). Finally, Vinciane Despret reflected on both: "it is through the grief one undergoes that life comes to matter; it is by accepting this grief that it counts. Taking the risk of vulnerability by facing up to grief so that vulnerable lives do not count for nothing, so that they 'count as lives'" (Despret 2016, 86). In light of the frequency of the euthanasia acts performed by zoo vets, one must ask what kind of challenges they present to the veterinarian's mental state in the long run. How might vets care for their own health?

Although the otter and the crane were handled by the same veterinarian in the same accredited zoo facility, the decision-making processes pertaining to how to care for, and whether to euthanize, these two animals were starkly different. The reasons for this difference are multiple and are mainly based on the relationship between the institution and the specific animal. Unlike the otter, the crane was not brought into captivity by the zoo, and so the zoo did not see itself as responsible to care for him for the duration of his life, according to Staggs. Avni-Magen of the Jerusalem Zoo further explained from a slightly different perspective that "managing *in situ* populations with agriculture damages and disease outbreak is much more accepted by the public and they can rationally understand it. But once you have a zoo animal, you are seen as responsible for its individual health" (interview).

Additionally, a wild animal cannot be as closely monitored as a zoo animal—so the range of medical interventions that the vet can perform in such cases are more limited. In the words of Horowitz from the Ramat Gan Safari Zoological Center, who functions as both the chief veterinarian for the zoo and as the director of the wildlife hospital jointly managed by the zoo and Israel's nature and parks authority: "If the gazelle's pup is limping, I won't be able to return it to the wild because it won't survive there for more than 20 minutes. But if it's going to the zoo, then it can limp as much as it wants. If a zoo animal is old, or our elephant is without teeth, we will accommodate and we will cut his food smaller for him. But if this were a wild elephant, he would need to be culled" (interview). Of 5,500 wild animals that arrive at the gates of Israel's wildlife hospital every year (some 15 animals daily), approximately one third are euthanized (Horowitz, interview).

Taking a similar stance, Endre Sós of the Budapest Zoo, who is both the vet for the zoos' animals and also runs the zoo's rescue center, told me that "at the zoo we don't kill geriatric animals as long as we can keep them in proper conditions. It's an artificial environment." However, he continued, "if you work in a wildlife hospital where you have animals which are coming from the wild, then your goal is to release them back to the wild." He further explained that, "Because these animals come from the wild, . . . it's a very stressful situation for them to be in a captive environment. So it becomes a welfare issue to actually keep them alive." Of the 2,201 animals the Budapest Zoo took into its rescue center last year, about one third were euthanized (interview).

Yet despite the formal adherence to the distinction between zoo and wild animals, in practice Sós goes out of his way not to kill healthy animals, even when they are not zoo animals. In his words: "I would kill a [rescue] bird without hesitation if there was a missing limb or something like that. But a bird that looks healthy and [just] because of her behavior cannot be released—if she's not suffering I'll keep her in captivity. I probably wouldn't kill her but I'd try to use her for a good purpose, like education" (interview). Alongside the general standards and principles about when to kill animals, cultural approaches and personal preferences and orientations make for multitude applications in practice.

After the crane was euthanized, Staggs took me for lunch at SeaWorld's staff cafeteria. She wanted to share at that point why she has chosen to work as a veterinarian in SeaWorld, and emphasized time and time again that she would never work at a zoo that did not have a stranding program (Vogelnest of the Taronga Zoo told me that marine mammals have been subject to more rescue projects than any other taxon). At her prior job, Staggs rescued 1,800 stranded turtles stunned by a cold spell and cared for them until it was warm enough to release them back, she told me. Shortly after, she was part of the team that performed the cleanup of the BP oil spill in the Gulf of Mexico. Here is her account of the "de-oiling" process:

> The [fishermen would] go out in the morning and they would bring the [animals] back at night when it started to get dark. All these animals that they had collected off the oil slicks would come into our facility. So the whole day we were caring for the animals that have already been de-oiled and treated. And then at night, we would get a new round. We ended up doing 156 turtles.... We had to radiograph every single turtle, check them for pneumonia, check them for oil ingestion, and then continue. It wasn't just one de-oiling process; we had to de-oil them several times. We actually gave them fish oil to bind with any oil in their digestive track. But then we couldn't just dump [the oil] into the water system. We had to build a completely different system for the contaminated water to be properly disposed of. And so we had the EPA in there looking at our systems, and then the CDC came in, too, to look at the workers who were doing this and wanting to draw our blood. And I remember the CDC workers looking at me and going, "You're pregnant." And I'm like, "Yeah."

Staggs preferred not to talk much about the personal sacrifices that her job as a zoo veterinarian entailed and the impacts that it has had on her family life. Yet the topic resurfaced in the context of her current work at SeaWorld, where she is part of an emergency rescue team that travels around the country to aid stranded dolphins, sea turtles, and sea lions. Scott Gass, Director of Communications at SeaWorld, joined our conversation at that point. Here is how it unfolded:

> LS: The nice thing about SeaWorld is that we are a critical care facility, one of only four in the State of Florida. So if there's an animal that needs to get rehabbed around this area, then most likely it's coming to us. We have the biggest facility [and] we have the largest number of vets, as well as experienced people, who care for these animals.
> IB: So you never say no?
> SG: We don't. And our team works 24 hours a day. We have an on call veterinary crew every night. Tomorrow, we could get a call to go up to South Carolina. We have the boats, we have the equipment, we have the nets, and we've got to take a vet. [So] we will get a team together.
> IB: Wow. [To Staggs:] And then you just leave home for a few days?
> LS: Yeah, yup.
> SG: [We] have somebody who carries a "bird phone" and they get multiple calls every day from citizens throughout Orlando who see a bird that needs care. Do we go out every single time? No, because, obviously, there's stuff in the park that we have to deal with when it comes to our own rescued animals. But we try to get there and help out the animals as best we can. And that goes for a bird, turtle, manatee, or dolphin.
> IB: So you're sort of like a hospital for stranded wildlife?
> SG: I cannot tell you the last time we said no to an animal. It's been years.
> IB: How can you do that? Aren't there more and more human-caused injuries to animals in the wild?
> LS: This [gestures toward the theme park rides, IB], pays for that. Every ticket, every stuffed animal, everything that you see here. This is what supports it. Come meet the ambassador animals—help pay for the rescues. Because SeaWorld doesn't

get government subsidies to do turtle rehab and to do wild bird rehab, they pay for it out of their own pocket.

IB: So if the sandhill crane [you euthanized earlier] was able to recover. Would you be doing the rehab here?

SG: Yeah. And in fact, just earlier this week a bird came in with a monofilament line wrapped around its foot. The bird was hobbling around, [but] we were able to get it cut off. It was probably here for two or three weeks and it got cleared. We took it back to where we found it. We had a bunny come in a couple of weeks ago. A squirrel, too. The other thing is that if someone shows up at the gate with a bird, we'll go up there and meet them and take it off their hands, no questions asked. We're not going to let that animal sit and suffer.

While the majority of zoo veterinarians still works strictly with zoo animals, many of the veterinarians I interviewed for this book—and the aquarium veterinarians in particular—emphasized the importance of their work in caring for wild animals in need, either when they are *in situ* or when they are cared for by the zoo through its rescue and rehabilitation capacity. In the words of veterinarian Sharon Deem of the Saint Louis Zoo: "We have a responsibility to provide good health and welfare for the animals under our care, but increasingly . . . we also have a responsibility to apply our training to animals that are 'free living'" (interview). The active form of caring for wild animals that occurs outside the zoo is yet another dimension of the transformation in the role and mindset of zoo veterinarians from individual welfare toward conservation management.

But the work of the zoo veterinarian with *in situ* wild animals has been quite challenging. The less fun aspects of this work are most evident when the zoo veterinarian rescue team must euthanize stranded animals in the wild. According to one of the vets I interviewed, who requested not to be identified in this context, such events have resulted in threats from certain animal rights activists toward them and their family. Assistant veterinarian Melissa Joblon of the New England Aquarium described similar threats. Here is her account of one such occurrence:

MJ: We have the largest sea turtle rescue hospital on the East Coast. . . . This past year, for example, we had over 470 turtles come through our facility within two months. . . . We get cold stunned animals here: they come in up through the Gulf and then, if the water temperature changes drastically, they can't get out in time. And they're reptiles, so they physiologically can't function beyond a certain cold temperature. So, they wash up on shore and either they die or we rescue them. . . . We used to average maybe 70 animals a year. [But] within the past 5 years or so, we're in the four hundreds. We had one year, where we had over 700 animals. So yes, it is getting worse. There is a recent paper out that is trying to predict how many animals will be coming in the future, how the water temperature is going to change and what risk factors are involved. They [predicted that] within 5 to 10 years, we will have over 2,000 animals in here.

IB: Do you release them after they get over their shock?

MJ: A lot of our work is to triage and try to get them stabilized and moved down south to different facilities where they are treated longer term, and we keep the sickest ones.

IB: So you don't release them where you found them?

MJ: Not usually. If they get through winter with us, sometimes we'll release them up here. But usually, we send them further south. [Admittedly,] we don't know a lot of the long term data about these animals. But are we going to let thousands of animals just die on the beach? . . . That being said, you can't save everyone, right? There are only a certain number of animals we can house comfortably, so if we see another animal on the beach, we'd need to let nature take its course. We get a lot of backlash, right? Then it's all of a sudden "the aquarium doesn't care." When I worked at the Mystic Aquarium, I've been through several dolphin strandings where I'd have to go and assess the animal. Most of the time, when a single dolphin is stranded by itself in an unusual area, it's that something is really physiologically wrong with it. It's a sick animal. I remember this one time, it was one of my first strandings that I attended as the primary vet. I remember assessing the animal. He had these giant lacerations. He was bleeding, very neurologic, not healthy. So we euthanized it. We noticed people yelling at us from the beach: "Dolphin killers! You don't care about these animals!" Do you think that I went to school for 8 years to come and just kill animals? That's the least favorite part of my job. It's heart-breaking, it's horrible. But what do you want me to do here? Let the animal just suffer for hours? Sometimes the public opinion gets a little skewed.

As the conversation with Joblon proceeded, the tough decisions facing the new generation of zoo veterinarians who work beyond the zoo walls, and the complex factors they must negotiate in their role as caregivers for a growing number of imperiled animals, populations, and habitats, became increasingly apparent. Whereas Joblon believes in the educational role of zoos, she also thinks that it is important to keep wild animals in captivity so that scientists may build knowledge and gain valuable skills that are important for *in situ* conservation. But while many zoos have developed guidelines and procedures about killing the zoo animals inside their gates, decisions about whether and when to intervene in the wild seem to occur in an ad hoc fashion, following few, if any, standards. Here is Joblon's account on both the educational and the research aspects of her work:

> MJ: I can understand why people can be uncomfortable with animals in captivity. When you see these large animals in what looks like a cage or a bathtub, it's definitely disheartening. But if you stop and talk to people who are doing this, you realize that . . . it's not just about capturing animals and putting them on display. Maybe in the past that was our only real goal. But now most zoos and aquariums, especially the ones that are AZA-accredited, have a goal of conservation education. Our true goal here is to inspire people, [and so we] show these animals. It does sound a little cheesy, right? But that, really, is the goal. If you stop and think about what we can learn from these animals in a managed setting, in a zoo or aquarium, what we learn about their anatomy, their physiology, [and] their behavior—that's how we're able to help animals in the wild. And again, sometimes that's why we criticize ourselves, especially veterinarians, when we do wildlife work and [there are] these mass stranding events. We can't avoid asking ourselves if helping these few individuals is helping the population. Maybe not. But as veterinarians, this is what we're trained to do and how we care.
>
> IB: Why wouldn't you be helping the species by saving the individual dolphins?
>
> MJ: So take for example some seals that come in that have pneumonia or a wound from a shark or something. Should we just let nature take its course? Maybe we should. But then we see the other individuals that are entangled in fishing gear, that

have ingested plastic or foreign material, or that got hit by a boat. So, we can't just do nothing about that, right?
IB: So where is the boundary between when you intervene and when you don't intervene? Is it only with human-induced injuries?
MJ: That's the thing. Right now, we don't have that [kind of boundary]. We try to help everything we can. Then again, that's where there is backlash from activists. They're unhappy that we're not helping the one individual that is clearly sick.
IB: Helping by making it live somehow?
MJ: Right, yes.
IB: But from your perspective, you do help them by saving them from their suffering, right? You don't let them suffer for many hours?
MJ: Sometimes I have to, though. If we can't get to that animal, it's not safe for us to go out there and disrupt all the other animals and then try to get back. It's not really a good use of our time, unless we know we can do something.

Because of their growing engagement with *in situ* wildlife, many zoo veterinarians must now make decisions about situations that occur outside of the zoo. In this context, the distinction between wild and zoo animals, and the role of zoo veterinarians as caring first and foremost for their institutions' animals, are no longer as clear-cut as they may have been in the past (if they ever were; on the eroding distinction between *in situ* and *ex situ* conservation, see Braverman 2015). And while many zoo veterinarians are increasingly involved in rescue and rehabilitation missions, others insist that the *in situ* versus *ex situ* animal boundary should not be blurred and that zoo vets should only, or mainly, care for their captive zoo animals. In Bertelsen's words: "I think we should leave animals alone when they're out there. Millions, if not billions, of wild animals die every day. We neither could nor should deal with that. It really isn't our problem."

In our conversation, Walzer of the Wildlife Conservation Society also mentioned some of the novel dilemmas facing zoo veterinarians who work in the rescue and rehabilitation of animals in the wild. He was concerned about what he perceived as the lack of conservation awareness on the part of the vets who work in this context. In his words: "They pick it up, they feed it, and they put it back in again—[but] they [don't always] think about what impacts that has on the population." By removing or rehabilitating birds of prey, for example, "you're actually removing the selective pressure on that population." From Walzer's perspective, then, certain animal species should not be subject to rehabilitation in the first place, and veterinarians should refuse to care for members of these species. As an example, he spoke about one year when the barn owl population exploded. That year, he treated five owls after they were hit by cars. "[But] I would not rehab them," he told me, explaining that "the landscape is saturated in those times, and the food is the limiting factor, so they get pushed out and they end up on the road. There's no point sending them out there again" (interview).

While he agreed with Walzer in principle, Vogelnest of the Taronga Zoo in Sydney was softer in his practice. When we communicated, he was in the midst of dealing with the catastrophic impact of the Australian wildfires on the region's vast ecosystems and wildlife populations. In response, he established triage centers and trained vets on how to treat burns, especially on koalas. An estimated one billion or more wild animals have died in the fires, and yet the number of rescues has been surprisingly low. "The exact number is still to be determined," Vogelnest told me. "But most of the animals have died" (interview).

The rescue efforts, too, have been far from simple, revealing the tensions between various groups about how to care for animals, "something vets often get caught in the middle of." "You've got this whole range of views on what should be done," Vogelnest said. And while it is illegal to save invasive species in Australia, and animals in this category are therefore euthanized on the spot, species that are abundant in numbers present a more complicated case for the conservation-minded vet. In the words of Vogelnest:

> It can be quite challenging for vets when we know that a particular animal should be euthanized, but we're dealing with someone who has a different philosophy. We have to be very careful over how we approach those situations. Koalas, for example, were introduced to Kangaroo Island, and there were thousands of them—[to the point that] the South Australian government spends hundreds of thousands of dollars contracepting these koalas [and others] on an annual basis. When large numbers died in the fires, ecologists were going: "Wow, okay. That's a good thing." But when we were working in

those areas and people were rescuing koalas . . . I don't think any vet would be brave enough to just say, "Hey, this koala shouldn't be on Kangaroo Island. Let's just euthanize it."

The responsibility of zoo veterinarians toward zoo animals vis-à-vis animals in the wild, and their decisions regarding when and where to intervene, which are always already dependent on permits from the relevant wildlife authorities, deserve further discussion at a time when a growing number of animals in the wild are requiring more intense intervention and management for their survival. As the pressures from the "outside" world are forcing the zoo walls to become more inclusive, zoo veterinarians must care for wild animals infiltrating into the zoo. At the same time, as vets "go wild," the entire wild world becomes implicated with the zoo's logic of bio-management. The wild versus zoo distinction is increasingly challenged and, in turn, challenges traditional veterinary expertise. A more holistic approach—one that encompasses zoo and wild animals as well as humans and that is rooted in an understanding of our codependence upon one another within the context of healthy ecosystems—is called for, if we are to heal this imperiled planet.

Euthanasia of Healthy Zoo Animals

Circling from *in situ* deliberations back to the zoo context, former executive director of EAZA Lesley Dickie estimated in 2014 that 3,000 to 5,000 animals are "management-euthanized" by European zoos in any given year (BBC 2014). While the 340 zoos that are accredited by EAZA must sign on to the association's various breeding programs, each practices its own discretion about management-based euthanasia. EAZA's 2014 Standards for the Accommodation and Care of Animals in Zoos and Aquaria (approved on September 27, 2014 and then revised and approved on April 25, 2019) provide the baseline that each member institution must abide by. Here are the mandatory 2014 EAZA standards that pertain to euthanasia for non-medical reasons:

3.3 Euthanasia
Euthanasia as a structural solution for undesired surplus animals may be acceptable under certain conditions beyond veterinary indication, such as the following:

1. Animals that can/may no longer make a breeding contribution, for example, because of old age, genetic overrepresentation of the possession of undesirable inheritable genetic traits.
2. Young animals born despite reproduction-limiting measures or recommendations that have been recently born, have reached weaning age or another age in which they would naturally leave the parent(s) or natal group.
3. Incompatibility of an animal with its conspecifics.
4. Hybrids and animals of an unknown or undefined subspecies in cases in which this is considered of importance.
5. Animals that are more dangerous than is reasonably expected.
6. Animals that despite changes in conditions (e.g., institution/enclosure/diet) continue to display abnormal behaviour or extraordinary timidity.
7. Animals that for some reason cannot otherwise be placed in suitable facilities.
8. Donated or otherwise acquired injured rehabilitation animals (EAZA 2019).

Whereas the European zoo standards permit zoos and their veterinarians to kill their animals for non-medical reasons ("beyond veterinary indication"), many zoos prefer not to attract public attention to such practices. The Copenhagen Zoo and its chief veterinarian Mads Bertelsen are vocal supporters of "management euthanasia," which zoo professionals often refer to as "culling." For Bertselsen, the definition of culling is "a planned and rational reduction of [an animal] population." Here is how he explained his approach:

> For many veterinarians trained to cater to the survival of the individual animal and used to contributing to species conservation one case at a time, it sometimes takes an effort to step back and see the bigger picture, where it is the long-term health and survival of the *population* that counts. The population has become the patient, and that patient is not doing so well (Bertselsen 2019, 134; emphasis in original).

Clearly, Bertelsen cares about the health of his nonhuman patient. However, the identity of this patient has changed: it is no longer the individual animal but the collective population. Like many other veterinarians, at the start of his career he was focused on saving individual animals, Bertelsen told me. Since then, however, "I gradually shifted so now I am there for the species and for the animals in general, more than for the individual. And that is very much reflected in some of my thoughts on euthanasia." Bertelsen is thus quite critical of the oft-used phrase that zoo vets "save species one individual at a time." His response:

> To me, this is nonsensical. Because sometimes those efforts are actually blocking the bigger picture. You're working on that individual, which I do on a daily basis. But what is it that counts? You can't let your affection for that individual cloud the decisions that you should be making in terms of the group or the species. This is where it sounds totally cold and unemotional, but for most of these animals, if you castrate it or sterilize it, or it's already non-reproductive for some other reason, then it no longer matters what a nice animal it is—it is dead to the population. It has no impact anymore. And there are very few exceptions, [such as] an old elephant that might play a social role in the group or something. But, in general, it is just taking up space for another animal, it takes physical resources, nutritional resources, and veterinary resources from where we should be putting our focus.

"I see myself first and foremost as a conservationist, and only then as a veterinarian," Bertelsen concluded.

Nonetheless, and although he rationally supports managerial killing, Bertelsen also recognizes the toll of such actions on his emotional state. He shared, accordingly, that "medical euthanasia is often a very satisfactory thing to do [because] we're giving this animal peace." However, "when you are culling an animal because it's in surplus, it's not a nice thing to do." It feels different from ending a life that needs ending, he continued. "This is the life that doesn't necessarily need ending, but [for which] that was the most rational thing to do under the circumstances." Bertelsen then proceeded to describe the routine culling practices at his zoo, using the management of the lion population as an example. In his words,

> We breed our lions every year or two, whatever the cycle is. And if we have too many, we will cull them. So when people

need lions, they come to us. . . . It became a somewhat irrational supply and demand thing because many zoos are concerned about culling. But basically, we do it for two reasons. First of all, if we don't breed animals, we'll suddenly run out. Right now some 70 percent of the programs in the United States are unsustainable. That means that they will either collapse or will need to import animals in the foreseeable future. That's the first reason. The other one is that lions are social cats. They live in big groups where they have offspring. [So this is how we] keep our animals healthy.

Whereas the first reason that Bertelsen listed for managing lion populations through culling has to do with the sustainability of animal populations at zoos, the second is based on the welfare of the individual zoo animals. Rather than focusing on the welfare of the animal who is killed, however, the focus here is on the behavioral needs of the parents and the social group, the idea being that the young animals will provide enrichment for that group until it is time to cull them. "From a purely rational perspective, the decision to breed and then cull young adult members for welfare purposes makes much more sense than how we manage animals in our zoos," Avni-Magen of the Jerusalem Zoo told me. "This is not some capricious or anti-humanitarian behavior on the part of northern European zoos that just love to kill their animals." Avni-Magen further explained that it is much healthier for a social group to live in similar patterns to what they would experience naturally, with the older adults dying out and the younger ones taking their place and leaving the group when they reached adulthood. "This allows us to diversify the genetics and the social relations among the group," she said.

At the same time, Avni-Magen also admitted that in Israel, "Our public and even our staff are not ready for this kind of zoo animal management." This might have something to do with the culture, or maybe it's religion, she relayed. "But here I can't even feed my carnivore animals the leg of a zebra if it looks like one." There is a lot of hypocrisy in this context, Avni-Magen concluded. Endre Sós of the Budapest Zoo agreed. "If you do total contraception, then of course it's neither good for the program nor is it good for the reproductive health of the animal." These animals in effect no longer contribute to the population and thus have no conservation value, he explained. "It's coming back to [animal rights] ethics and welfare versus conservation management," he explained. Yet despite this recognition, he told me, "we don't do 'breed and cull' here in Hungary." According to Walzer, "breed and cull" policies can be accurately traced along a geographic line. In his words:

> As you go further south, the veterinarians become more and more reluctant to euthanize animals and to consider that as an option for population management. [When] you go north to Austria and Germany, it's a bit of a mix: it's historically a problem to address euthanasia there. But when you go north from there, it becomes quite acceptable and an open and transparent discussion. In North America, these things happen as well, they're just not transparent and they're not open about it. They're lying. That's the modus operandi in the United States. It's just "let's not talk about it," which is quite different than some European countries.

Shortly before our interview, Bertelsen culled a male African lion at the Copenhagen Zoo for managerial reasons. A higher number of males are culled because they are less important for the sustainability of the zoo population, he explained. Here is his description of the procedure and his thoughts about how the lions perceived it:

> They were three out of a litter and they received the same dart by a blow pipe. They all fell asleep, [but only] one of them never woke up. The others woke up in a crate on the way to France. My point is that when they're still in their enclosure they don't know the difference. So they fall asleep, of course not knowing what's going to happen and, frankly, they don't even know that they're falling asleep. They just think "something hit me," and then they get drowsy and fall asleep. According to my ethics, that animal doesn't know any differently, [so] I don't have any problems with doing that. But, of course, I enjoyed the procedure of loading those two other animals and sending them off to serve the population much more than I did taking the life of the last one, even though I knew that this also served the population in the sense that it kept the wheels turning and it kept the group in a natural state of behavior as being part of the generational cycle.

How to interpret Bertelsen's attempt to "think like a lion" (if to borrow from Despret's "thinking like a rat")? Is it stemming from his reluctance to anthropomorphize the lion by assuming that the human's fear of death applies to him, or is it, rather, a scientification of this lion's lifeworld that makes it possible for Bertelsen to assume that the lion cannot sense his approaching death and thus that his welfare is not implicated? As Despret points out in the context of comparing chimpanzee and human mourning in ways that naturalize mourning (2016, 174), to imply that animals do not have an awareness of death is already anthropocentric as it imposes upon them a human interpretation of death.

Notably, African lions are not an imperiled species; they are therefore not managed among European zoos through a collective breeding program (or EEP). When I wondered about the conservation value of keeping this population in captivity in the first place, Bertelsen explained that this is done mainly for educational purposes. He also mentioned that lions might become threatened in the future, in which case they will already have an established insurance population in zoos, and knowledge about how to manage and care for them via captive breeding. "No zoo is perfect, but we're moving in the right direction," Avni-Magen added in this context (interview).

Another culling routine performed by the Copenhagen Zoo involves the fruit bat population, which amounts to 100 individuals who can breed up to 50 young per year. These newborn bats are placed on a surplus list so that the relevant institutions know that they are available for adoption. "But whoever is not placeable would then be euthanized," Bertelsen told me. "In conjunction," he added, "we would typically have researchers from various universities, together with our own research staff, harvest as much as possible from these animals to make the most out of them." Such "harvesting" practices include taking samples from every animal who dies at the zoo and adding this sample to the regional biobank. In North America, such a biobank has been operative for many years and is managed by the San Diego Zoo. In Europe, the effort is more recent and is managed through EAZA (EAZA Biobank n.d.).

Zoo animals thus serve as research subjects not only during their lifetime, but also after their death. Historian of medicine Abigail Woods observed along these lines that: "Doctors' interest in the health of zoo animals did not end with the failure of preventive

Figure 4.3 Veterinarian Nili Avni-Magen performs a necropsy procedure on a female fallow deer in the Sorek Valley in 2020. This deer was reintroduced from the Jerusalem Zoo and was monitored for one year when the GPS collar sent death signals. Avni-Magen explained that it was important for her to reach the deer before the jackals did so that she could learn about the deer's physical state after one year of living in the wild (text communication, January 26, 2020). Courtesy of the Jerusalem Zoo.

or curative interventions. After animals died, they awarded them additional roles as pathological specimens" (Woods et al. 2018, 43; see, e.g., Figure 4.3).

Back in Copenhagen, Bertelsen emphasized that the fruit bats are quite unusual in terms of the relatively large numbers routinely killed from this population. Not counting bats, he performs an average of one medical euthanasia and less than one management-based euthanasia per week. "We're not talking about culling elephants every week here," he stressed. Finally, the zoo also euthanizes animals from the wild. In his words: "Occasionally, somebody will bring me a squirrel or a pigeon that were injured on the [zoo] grounds or just outside and say, 'Can you help me?' And, of course, I will help if I can. But these are very low numbers."

Although we did not address this topic until the end of our interview, Marius the giraffe loomed in the background of our conversation the entire time. Despite the many years that have passed since his death, this event is etched in Bertelsen's mind. More than anything else, he is still frustrated with how the media portrayed the event. He was particularly upset that they told it as if the giraffe was a baby (he was a young adult), as if he was shot in public (he was not), and as if Danish children were inappropriately exposed to the necropsy (these were invited guests who were looking forward to the educational opportunity). "It was interesting to see how fast that [misinformation] spread around the globe and how many of the reactions were actually based on something that wasn't entirely true," Bertelsen recounted. More generally, this is what he took from the event:

> It really is fascinating how different cultures have different ways of looking at this. Nobody really got excited about this here in Denmark, but in the United States it was a big deal, [and also] in the UK. I was working in Saudi Arabia on oryx conservation at the time and the Prince in the Saudi Wildlife Commission [taunted] me, "Ah, here comes the criminal!" to which he immediately added: "I think you were absolutely right." The funny thing is [that] there are zoos in the Far East that will feed live goats and donkeys to their tigers and lions, and I am upset by that—I think it's totally unacceptable. And then there are people who probably feel exactly like that about the things that I'm saying and doing. Am I allowed to be enraged by some Midwest American burger-eating lady who will say: "How can you feed giraffe pieces to a lion, you should just buy some meat for it"? The vast majority of citizens in the United States are absolutely fine with cows being slaughtered and eaten. How could they get so [up in arms] about a giraffe, which is basically just a cow with a longer neck and legs? Clearly, it is the question of where we come from that determines our attitude toward animals.

Bertelsen's cynical comment about the "burger-eating lady" who doesn't see the double standard when criticizing his zoo for feeding the lions with giraffe flesh was echoed by Walzer of the Wildlife Conservation Society. In Walzer's words, "It's not a welfare issue if you shoot something through the middle of its head [and it] dies instantaneously. There is no pain involved. There is no fear involved. [By contrast,] that cattle that was killed so you could eat your burger probably went through a lot of fear and had a lot of stress before it died" (interview).

The double standards in myriad human dealings with nonhuman animals have also been highlighted in the posthumanities scholarship, which often applies Foucault's biopolitical framework to make sense of it. In *Before the Law: Humans and Other Animals in a Biopolitical Frame* (2012), philosopher Cary Wolfe presents two polarized examples of how nonhuman animals are currently framed with regard to both their moral standing and their legal protections. It is ironic, in his view, that the Spanish Parliament decided to grant human rights to great apes "at the very moment when the violence of biopolitics against 'the body of the world' has never been more virulent and more systematic, nowhere more so than in today's practices of factory farming" (Wolfe 2012, 104).

Similarly, Nicole Shukin's *Animal Capital* (2009) provides a chilling testimony to the unfathomable schism between how humans treat pet animals and how we treat industry farm animals. Drawing on Agamben's biopolitical framework, Shukin has argued that the modern industrial slaughterhouse is the zoopolitical equivalent of the Nazi concentration camp in that they have both produced "bare life" (2009, 10; see also Braverman 2018b). Judith Butler's juxtaposition between killable and grievable life (2004) is also helpful for explaining that what might seem like hypocrisy is, in fact, a very comprehensive and calculated normative hierarchy that distinguishes between different categories of animals, making some more grievable than others, what I refer to elsewhere as "zoometrics" (Braverman 2017). Such insights from what one might refer to as the medical posthumanities could be invaluable for One Health.

Another point of contention in the Marius event had to do with the treatment of his body. The international media was disturbed by the fact that after the necropsy, Marius was fed to the lions. But while it feeds giraffe flesh to the lions, the Copenhagen Zoo would not feed its culled lions to any other zoo animals. Bertelsen explained that "we know that a zebra can be fed to a lion—that's fine and natural. But a lion being fed to another lion, or a lion being fed to a tiger, might present disease risks. So we wouldn't do that." He reasoned that lions and tigers live in distinct geographies and so they would not mix in the wild. "We've seen it with primates," he continued. "When you have very healthy primates from all sorts of different species, if you mix the ones from South America with the ones from Asia, then you suddenly see weird diseases cropping up that you wouldn't have necessarily seen otherwise."

Despite the fact that most of the individual zoo animals have never lived anywhere near their geographies of origin, those still play an important role within the zoo environment. Here, again, a deeper understanding of animals emerges that moves beyond their individual identity to understanding them as multispecies that have evolved within an ecological context. This understanding resonates with the sensibilities of conservation medicine, EcoHealth, and One Health and is especially important in this age of epidemics, which requires from us a realization that each individual is also its own ecosystem—and a unique "pathogen package," to borrow from the words of veterinarian Sharon Deem.

Euthanizing Fish: A Regulatory Patchwork

The animals I have discussed thus far as subjects of euthanasia were mostly charismatic megafauna. Whereas the unspoken assumption for most of these animals has been that they feel pain and thus that caring for such animals includes managing their pain to the point of killing them, some animals have historically been excluded from this assumption. This includes "less-like-us" taxa such as fish. The questions that arise around fish euthanasia arguably illuminate the interconnections between pain, care, and death, which I started to discuss in Chapter 2.

"Veterinarians are trained to treat all animals equally," Nuno Pereira of the Lisbon Oceanarium emphasized in our conversations. For this reason, he continued, a veterinarian would never say, "Well, this is a sardine, I don't have anesthesia so let's use a hammer, or something like that." Instead, even though "the anesthetic is quite expensive, if I want to euthanize a sardine, I [will] use the same anesthetic that I would use to euthanize a [grouper]." The Animal Veterinary Medicine Association's 2013 Guidelines for the Euthanasia of Animals has adopted a similar approach. Using the "preponderance of the accumulated evidence" principle, these Guidelines state, broadly, that:

While there is ongoing debate about finfishes', amphibians', reptiles', and invertebrate animals' ability to feel pain or otherwise experience compromised welfare, they do respond to noxious stimuli. Consequently, the Guidelines assume that a conservative and humane approach to the care of any creature is warranted, justifiable, and expected by society. Euthanasia methods should be employed that minimize the potential for distress or pain in all animal taxa, and these methods should be modified as new taxa-specific knowledge of their physiology and anatomy is acquired (AVMA 2013, 13).

The Guidelines are quite specific about how this principle translates into action in veterinary work. As the following paragraph illustrates:

[T]he preparations for euthanasia of finfish should be very similar to the preparations for anesthesia of finfish. If possible, withholding food for 12 to 24 hours prior to euthanasia will reduce regurgitation, defecation, and nitrogenous waste production. The environment should be as quiet and non-stimulatory as possible given the circumstances. Light intensity should be reduced if possible. . . . Water quality should be similar to that of the environment from which the finfish originated, or optimized for that species and situation, for the duration of euthanasia. . . . If euthanizing a large population of finfish, it is important to monitor the anesthetic bath water quality (temperature, dissolved O_2, and organic loading, in particular). . . . Euthanasia methods should be tested in one animal or a small group of animals prior to use in a large population for an unfamiliar species. If handling is required, appropriate equipment (nets, gloves) should be used to minimize stressors (AVMA 2013, 68–69).

The level of detail provided in the Guidelines is stunning and contributes to a sense that euthanasia—literally, the "good death"—is at the same time also a hyperlegal and scrutinized one. This is especially evident in AVMA Appendices 2 and 3, which provide elaborate tables on accepted and unaccepted methods of euthanasia, with a breakdown to categories such as mode of action, rapidity, ease of performance, safety for personnel, efficacy, and species suitability for each agent. This meticulous attention to detail when it comes to the death of certain forms of life invites comparison with the lack of detail regarding the death of others. As veterinarian Véronique LePage of Ripley's Aquarium in Canada told me: "there are always the underdogs and, in the case of the veterinary standards, those are the invertebrates. Even if there is a standard [for invertebrates], there are no baselines to implement it in practice" (interview).

Broadly speaking, the veterinary standards assume that animal pain must be avoided or minimized, even at the cost of death. Such an avoidance of pain has been with us since the 19th century's animal welfare laws at least (Shmuely 2019). The term "humane endpoint," which was coined in the context of laboratory animals, has also been used in the zoo context. In the United States, the Department of Agriculture (USDA) is the agency charged with implementing the Animal Welfare Act of 1966. The USDA defines humane endpoints as points that are "chosen to minimize or terminate the pain or distress of the experimental animals via euthanasia rather than waiting for their deaths as the endpoint" (USDA n.d.; see also Humane Endpoints n.d.). Similarly, the European Convention for the Protection of Vertebrate Animals used for Experimental and other Scientific Purposes states that, "The well-being and state of health of animals shall be observed sufficiently closely and frequently to prevent pain or avoidable suffering, distress, or lasting harm" (Article 5). Finally, it provides that: "At the end of the procedure it shall be decided whether the animal shall be kept alive or killed by a humane method" (Article 11). As for fish, the guidelines regarding "humane endpoints" distinguish between the slaughter, killing, and euthanasia of this taxon (AVMA 2013; Yanong et al. 2007).

Because of the central role of veterinarians in the arenas of animal health and welfare, the AVMA Guidelines have become the required standard regarding animal euthanasia across the board. But while the use of the AVMA Guideline is appropriate for vets working with fish species in controlled settings, they have limited application in the wild, and some vets have thus called to use a different set of criteria and indications in such settings. For this reason and others, the standards pertaining to the euthanasia of fish have been referred to as a "patchwork of regulations and regulatory agencies" (Yanong 2007, 4). Critics of the AVMA Guidelines highlight in particular that these Guidelines have "caused confusion regarding outcomes and intentions of fish slaughter, killing, or euthanasia among many professionals working with fish" (Yanong 2007, 4).

Conclusion: Compassion Fatigue and Care for Oneself

This chapter has focused on animal killing by zoo and aquarium veterinarians. It started by exploring the traditional form of killing practiced by the veterinarian at the zoo: that which is performed for the medical welfare of the zoo animal herself. Most Western vets in accredited zoos seem to be in agreement about the use of euthanasia in such cases, yet they differ with regard to when and how to kill. The chapter has also shown that, although they still work mainly within the zoo walls, zoo veterinarians are increasingly expanding their care also to wild animals outside of the zoo. The norms that govern killing animals inside and outside the zoo differ greatly, I have shown here, even with regard to members of the same species. In most circumstances, the zoo animal is allowed to live longer, albeit under compromised conditions, while the wild animal is killed to prevent her further suffering.

The chapter has also explored acts of killing animals by veterinarians for population management purposes. This type of euthanasia—or "culling"—occurs even when the health of the individual animal is not compromised. Since acts of killing are routinely carried out by conservation managers in *in situ* contexts, ecologically-oriented veterinarians are more accustomed to such practices and do not necessarily see them as problematic. There are considerable geographic, cultural, and even personal differences in this regard. Some vets even go so far as to draw a geographic line above which "breed and cull" practices are utilized openly for the sake of the effective management of healthy zoo animal populations. As for "culling" animals in the wild for managerial purposes, here most zoo veterinarians I spoke with still feel uncomfortable, although a few are already sounding a more interventionist approach—holding, for example, that zoo vets should cull "invasive" species when those reach their wildlife rescue facilities. Finally, this chapter has turned its attention to fish to discuss how euthanasia is practiced and secured through the standardization and the regulation of the fine details of veterinary operations. The hyperlegal apparatus that has emerged around what is typically seen as the profession's most difficult decision—killing animals—reveals the challenges facing the contemporary work of zoo and aquarium veterinarians and the significance of regulation for the medical practice of caring for animals.

In closing, a final note on care. Largely, this chapter—and the entire book—has focused on zoo and wild animals as subjects of care. Every now and again, however, the zoo vet herself has emerged as a candidate for such care. Following his observation of veterinary work with British cattle, Science and Technology Studies scholar John Law distinguishes between four objects of veterinary care in that context: care for the animal, for the farmer, for various versions of collectivity, and for the self (Law 2010). As a step toward better caring for themselves, several of the zoo vets I have spoken with have acknowledged the emotional toll of their work, emphasizing that veterinarians have one of the highest suicide rates of any profession (see also Tomasi et al. 2019). Larry Vogelnest of the Taronga Zoo offered, along these lines, that "compassion fatigue [and] moral stress are huge issues for vets. For years they have gone unrecognized, but now these things are coming out." Vogelnest believes that euthanasia is one of the significant contributors to this compromised mental state: "Euthanizing animals—regardless of whether they are healthy, whether it's because of welfare reasons, or whatever—affects some more than others. And compassion fatigue is a very significant problem for a lot of people who care for wildlife" (interview).

This book has repeatedly offered that acts of caring should extend not only to all living animals—including humans and even vets—but also to other forms of life and to the earth herself, emphasizing the profound ways in which we are all connected.

Conclusion
Planet Doctors
One Health from Koalas to Coronavirus

> Day-to-day reality, the life we live, is also a fleshy affair. A matter of chairs and tables, food and air, machines and blood. Of bodies. That is a good reason not to leave these issues in the hands of medical professionals alone but to seek ways, *lay ways* so to speak, to freely talk about them.
> —Annemarie Mol, *The Body Multiple* (2002, 27)

The New Zoo Veterinarian

Several recent scholarly works have stressed the importance of bridging the gap between animal rights and ecological conservation in the Anthropocene. In "Animal Welfare and Conservation: An Essential Connection," anthrozoologist Paul Waldau argues that the dismissive attitude by certain conservationists toward animal rights stands in the way of the natural alliance between these two movements, which have many common interests and share many concerns (2011, 13; see also Callicott 1980). Legal scholar Jonathan Lovvorn, formerly Chief Counsel for the Humane Society of the United States, has similarly invited climate activists to learn from animal rights campaigns how to work effectively to bring about meaningful change on the climate front (2016, 63–64).

Relatedly, in his concluding essay in the collection *Ignoring Nature No More: The Case for Compassionate Conservation*, ecologist Marc Bekoff calls for compassion in our interactions with nature, which many see as a different way of promoting individual animal welfare. Following what he describes as a "moral imperative," and approaching conservation on a case-by-case basis, he argues that humans will soon recognize their interdependence with the rest of the ecosystem (2013, 387; see also Braverman 2018b).

Along these lines, scientists Paul Paquet and Chris Darimont have suggested a "wildlife welfare" ethic in conservation (Paquet and Darimont 2010). Focusing specifically on North American wildlife, they observe that the environmental destruction of habitats has resulted in animal welfare issues such as starvation, trauma, and death, and so they urge conservationists to engage more actively with animal welfare approaches (Paquet and Darimont 2010, 186; Braverman 2018b).

As much as they consider welfare an important aspect of their work, the proponents of medical conservation and One Health regard their efforts through a different lens than that of compassionate conservationists and wildlife welfarists. This book has repeatedly shown that the novel challenge facing the zoo veterinarians, who have been central to these initiatives, is not so much to inject more welfare into their conservation work, but rather to balance between multiple forms of health. Such health considerations move beyond what has traditionally been perceived as the exclusive scope of medical expertise—the individual body—to include the health of microbiomes, populations, and ecosystems, considerations that do not translate neatly into animal welfare agendas. Veterinarian Chris Walzer of the Wildlife Conservation Society highlighted a few of the practical implications of such differences:

> You always have to consider welfare, even in conservation actions. But compassionate conservationists tell us that we cannot cull rats from some island because they are just as valuable as the last remaining [member] of a bird [species] there. This drives me nuts. From my perspective, things are quite clear: we cannot compromise conservation [or] endangered species habitats to protect alien invasive species.

While acknowledging the importance of individual animal welfare (be it human or nonhuman), conservation medicine and One Health proponents have been critical of both traditional medical practitioners and animal welfare advocates, citing their single-minded focus and calling instead for a broader scope that includes ecological health.

A central node in this novel interdisciplinary conglomerate is epidemiology. Ecologist Richard Ostfeld was quoted saying in this context that conservation medicine has an important role to play in making explicit the linkages between wildlife veterinary medicine, conservation biology, and epidemiology. "There really hasn't been any unified field that combines these perspectives," he offered (quoted in Norris 2001, 8). Conservation medicine scientists can piece together an understanding of the processes—spanning all levels of biological organization, from cells to ecosystems—that comprise the ecological context of health. Such an approach is a radical shift away from viewing diseases solely in terms of the response of individual organisms to infection or the spread of infection through populations (8).

Working at the intersection of biomedicine and ecology, zoo veterinarians are ideally positioned to develop a more inclusive conservation medicine agenda. And while the collaborations between field veterinarians and ecologists "have been more the exception than the rule" (Norris 2001, 9), the size and influence of this small but active group of zoo veterinarians who are coordinating the health and conservation needs of various humans and nonhumans, micro- and macro-organisms, populations, and ecosystems is steadily growing. Equipped with algorithmic population management tools, novel PCR technologies, and scissors, this emerging cohort of zoo veterinarians has become the vanguard of One Health. Uniquely situated at the nexus of wild, zoo, and the domestic human–animal worlds, zoo vets bridge between these worlds—serving as the front line caretakers of a diseased planet. Walzer clarified:

> Traditional livestock disease management works with fences, boundaries, [and] legislation. But that really only works so far. . . . We need to have a more holistic approach to livestock diseases, which includes the environment [and] climate change. So we are shifting now. All these things are now being integrated. And one of the things that we are also understanding is resilient landscapes. We need to have landscapes where the communities have more resilience, [where] they can adapt. And we are having this whole discussion at the moment about vaccination and herd immunity. So it's an interesting time (interview).

Categories that were once perceived as more or less bounded are increasingly understood by One Health proponents as messy, fluid, and dynamic interspecies relationships (Haraway 2003, 2008; Tsing 2012).

But does the One Health approach go far enough? Does it indeed challenge the boundaries—not only between disciplines and expertise, but also between humans, animals, systems, and everything in between? In "Views from Many Worlds," social anthropologists Hayley MacGregor and Linda Waldman suggest that it does not. Stressing the importance of anthropological perspectives to conservation medicine, they assert that:

> One Health ideas are based on an assumption of interconnectedness and intersectoral interaction, but this must be taken a step further to acknowledge ontologies where relevant categories such as nature and culture are perceived in radically different ways. This involves closer attention to people's own knowledge about the nature of relationships between humans and animals, as well as to the implications of how people "think with" and "think about" animals in different contexts. If we can bring this kind of knowledge into One Health debates, we find ourselves with a multiplicity of worldviews where we cannot presuppose bounded categories, and where the interfaces and interactions between these can be reconceptualized in terms of the social and relational. This might in turn influence our scientific ways of seeing our own disciplinary cultures, enabling fresh conversations and an unsettling of taken for granted assumptions and boundaries (2017, 7).

In other words, MacGregor and Waldman contend that although One Health speaks about multiplicity and cross-disciplinarity, it is at the same time reliant on Western scientific ways of knowing and practicing medicine and on traditional distinctions between humans and animals and between nature and society. They show, for example, that the vast majority of One Health texts do not incorporate Indigenous vocabularies or insights about colonial structures and ethnic, racial, or gender power dynamics.

This, perhaps, is what a social science and posthumanities participation could bring to One Health: a fresh perspective that would productively unsettle the categories implied by One Health frameworks and the boundaries they still all-too-readily draw between humans, animals, and the environment. "Human exceptionalism blinds us," anthropologist Anna Tsing wrote (2012, 144), in a statement that is not only descriptive but also cautionary. Despite its blind spots, however, it is important to acknowledge that the One Health approach promoted by a growing number of zoo veterinarians is at the forefront of this powerful and potentially transformative moment. It teaches us that the way forward is by drawing the connections and bridging the divides. The humanists and social scientists among us can help craft a medical posthumanities approach that would advance us one more step toward bridging these divides.

Human–Animal Boundaries Revisited

I keep reliving this moment: I am lying on the concrete floor of the wildlife clinic—bleeding, shivering, suffering—and being ignored by the zoo's veterinarian, who continues to care for the lizard in front of her. This happened to me as a human—and precisely *because* I am a human. As someone who has closely observed and documented the marginalization of nonhuman animals, this occurrence has come as a blow. What happened here? And was what happened as nonsensical as it seemed to me at first?

The answer is complex, and illuminates the strong divide between species that arguably still rules the veterinary profession, in zoos and beyond. Indeed, when I have asked zoo veterinarians across the world about the human–nonhuman divide, many of them justified it. Bertselsen from Copenhagen explained, half-jokingly, that he wouldn't want to take care of humans because "they complain too much," while Memarian from Tehran suggested that caring for humans requires a different set of skills and expertise, and Vogelnest noted that in Australia it is in fact illegal for a vet to care for humans. When I attended the monthly physical checkup of orcas at SeaWorld (which included weighing, urine and blood tests, and a dental exam), I couldn't help but wonder how many humans on this planet experience this level of intimate and regular health care—ever. As if reading my thoughts, the orcas' lead trainer told me: "If you want me to be honest, they get better health care than me." Walzer of the Wildlife Conservation Society put it even more bluntly:

> You'd have to drag me into a human hospital. I will always first go to my veterinary colleagues and get treated. First of all, it's much faster. If I need to just stitch up from trauma or something like that, why would I bother going down and sitting three hours in the emergency room when I could have it done in five minutes?

Walzer has worked for many years in Austria, where the veterinary staff cared for each other. But he has encountered a very different experience since moving to New York. "I've really noticed a complete [human–animal] separation in North America," he told me. When his ear hurt, for example, he went down to the veterinary clinic to get it checked. "My ear only had to be looked inside, which is something we did in [Austria] all the time. But they were really shocked that I was asking them to do that. I was like, 'C'mon, just look inside, see if it looks inflamed.'" The vet eventually yielded and performed the exam. "I was very grateful and everything," Walzer recounted. "But I got this extremely long disclaimer that he's not a medical doctor and that although he doesn't see anything, there's no guarantee. I was quite curious—I hadn't realized this was such a big deal."

More generally, Walzer also shared his thoughts about medical care for humans in the United States. "If you treated a dog like that, you'd lose your license. It's completely unacceptable," he said point blank. Science and Technology Studies scholar Bruno Latour commented along these lines: "Deprived of the attention given to them by other "companion species," humans have lost the ability to behave as humans. This is what renders the fight against anthropomorphism so ironic: today most humans are not treated by sociologists or economists as generously as wolves, ravens, parrots, and apes are treated by their scientists" (in foreword to Despret 2016, xiii–xiv).

Relatedly, when reintroducing the Asian wild ass in rural East Asia, Walzer found it impossible to maintain a human–nonhuman separation in medical care. He reflected:

> Every single one of those animals would be treated for everything because they were very valuable. So we had a really good facility there to care for them—we had all the drugs and everything we needed. And we were definitely the best medical facility for hundreds of kilometers. So once a week we'd have humans lining up for help, too. This was a few years after the collapse of the Soviet Union—there was nothing else then. So we were taking care of everyone there. I'd be on the phone [with my physician friends] in a hospital and I'd say, "Okay, I have this person sitting here, what do you want me to do?" And they would tell me, "Okay, do this, do that and then treat this and that." Crazy days.

Conclusion 129

When I briefly told him about my accident, Walzer's response was uncompromising. "I'm appalled," he said bluntly. "There's no excuse for that." "I don't think this could have happened in any European institution," he continued. "Ever." Walzer then proceeded to explain, more generally, that:

> Especially when you fall over, you're normally bleeding quite a bit. And so as a vet, you do want to check what's going on—and the lizard can wait. Honestly, people have a completely wrong understanding of the legal implications. Someone on the floor for a half an hour might actually result in much more serious legal implications because you are not providing this person with first aid. As wildlife veterinarians, we are faced with even more difficult situations because first aid is not enough for us—we actually need to be trained to provide much more help. I'm in places where it could take five days or more for any [physician] to come and help. Add to that the dangers we're under: if we do a bad job and the animal [we're working with] gets us. That's one thing. But mostly it's accidents with cars, motorcycles, the drugs we administer—there's a lot of things that can go wrong. So we need to have an agreed upon way for helping each other. When I go into the field with a group, we will normally sit down and have a discussion and everyone basically agrees that you do what you can to help. I've been in situations in zoos as well where, in hundreds and hundreds of rhino anesthesia, there are those two or three cases where someone was inattentive and got crushed and their foot was broken. The first thing you need to do is to get that person safely stabilized. And depending how fast help comes, you need to be more and more invasive.
>
> I [also] had a mixed animal practice. . . . And I remember two occasions with men who fainted outright. One fell onto the ground and nothing much happened, but the other fell onto a radiator and just caught the corner with his head. There was a massive puddle of blood everywhere. His child was traumatized. You can't just leave the person lying on the ground, bleeding. You give the cat a bit more anesthesia and then provide first help to the poor man.
>
> Then there were the Cesarean sections on cattle. Have you witnessed any of those? The cow is not even under full anesthesia—it

[might just be] standing there, eating in the barn, but it has a 30 or 40-centimeter-large hole at its side, from where you pull the calf out. You have the farmers helping you. And it was a well-known fact that all the farmers who were also working in the slaughterhouse, who were butchers, would instantaneously faint. They could not deal with blood when the animal was alive. They were quite capable of killing hundreds of cattle per day, but they couldn't handle cutting anything that's alive. I was always surprised. I learned that from my mentor as a young vet. He instructed me to always ask if anyone is a butcher, and if they were, to make sure they were standing at the head of the cow, so they couldn't see what was going on. If you'd show them the wound, they'd fall right into it.

Admittedly, Walzer's list of humans who, like me, "lost it" during a bloody animal procedure made me feel slightly less embarrassed about my own fall. But this personal realization should also serve to underline the potentially powerful contribution that conservation medicine and One Health has to offer by challenging the human–animal divide. This understanding was articulated by the physician Rudolf Virchow in the 1800s. In his words: "Between animal and human medicine, there is no dividing line—nor should there be" (quoted in Deem 2018, 699).

Zoo Veterinarians reflected on the reversal of the object–subject divide, when humans, because of their ability to talk (and complain—or sue), are treated more like objects, whereas animals, who are valued in their wildness and authenticity, are treated humanely. Whereas the legal distinction between human and animal care was likely developed in order to protect humans, bringing down the divide means also reflecting on the varying standards of medical care applied across the species gradient. I would like to use my own traumatic experience to exemplify the pitfalls of a rigid adherence to the human–animal divide. And one of the first things I had learned from the accident is what it feels like to be the species that is not the subject of care—which is ironic, because the division was intended to prioritize humans.

My view of the accident has certainly changed over time: from embarrassment and anger ("how foolish of me! Still, why are they ignoring me and lavishing care on the lizard?"), through an understanding of the veterinarians' stance of professional detachment and the clinical lens they deploy ("vets should care for animals and doctors for humans, while lawyers should enforce that division"), to a posthumanist critique ("the human–animal divide and its materialities should be examined critically"). But even beyond questioning the specific distinctions between human and nonhuman animals, we should reevaluate the varying modes of care applied to living organisms, including those without vertebrates and those who are too tiny for humans to see. Medical experts should see beyond such distinctions if they are to successfully care for the interconnected array of life that exists on our diseased planet.

Finally, one must not forget the importance of ethnographic perspectives and the transformative practice of meddling. Annemarie Mol contends along these lines:

> Doctors talking about their work may be listened to as if (like patients) they were their own ethnographers; ethnographers in their turn need not stop short as soon as they come across machines or blood, but can continue their observations. They may write about the body and its diseases. I will attend to physicalities even if I am not a medical doctor. To understand that it can be done. That there are ways of ethnographically talking bodies (2002, 27).

Although Mol's central concerns in this text are situated mainly in the medical humanities (she studies medical professionals and human patients), her insights are highly relevant here as well. The question is: what exactly happens when medical experts care for the health of *nonhuman* animal patients? And can we begin to envision such experts also attending to the health of the planet?

Zoo Veterinarians Triaging Care

As I wrote this book's final words in January 2020, the fires that have ravaged large parts of Australia were finally dying out, leaving behind over one billion dead wild animals and an inconceivable destruction of vast social and ecological systems. At the same time, a new zoonotic disease referred to as coronavirus has been identified, its epicenter in Wuhan, China. The source of this disease seems to have been a "wet" animal market, where dead and living animals were sold side-by-side (Deem, interview). Whereas these two events, which occurred in the course of a single month, seem unrelated, I am interested in what relating them to each other tell us about the role that zoo veterinarians can—and should—perform in this age of extinction and, furthermore, what this can tell us about the shift in our conceptions of care during times of crisis.

In January 2020, veterinarians from across the country and from around the world came together in Australia to treat wildlife affected by the fires, which were likely exacerbated by the droughts and higher temperatures of climate change. As these circumstances impact organisms and ecosystems across the planet, the role of the zoo vet in caring for wild animals—as individuals, as populations, and within their broader environmental context, while also triaging who to make live and who to let die—is becoming more and more apparent, too.

When koala rescue centers saw a rapid influx of thousands of burned animals, zoo vets came to act as translators, teaching vets who have limited experience with wild animals not only *how* to attend to the wounds, but also how to assess *whether* to attend to them. "These decisions need to be made quickly," veterinarian Larry Vogelnest from the Taronga Zoo told me. He had just finished designing an online training manual to facilitate the growing demands more effectively. "Vets who don't have much experience with wildlife can quickly look at this one-hour training resource and get some basic knowledge on how to deal with burnt wildlife," he said. But an even more important part of this triage process, he added, is to determine whether to treat the animal in the first place. In his words: "You really want to focus your resources on the animals that are most likely to survive, [rather than] spend a lot of time trying to save an animal that's unlikely to survive. That's the whole principle of triaging with animals." Vogelnest also explained the surprisingly low number of animal patients that have reached the rescue centers during and after the fires: "Many more animals have died than could be rescued, for sure" (see, e.g., Figure C.1).

This has been a trying time for zoo veterinarians. Vets with a conservation orientation have been doubly traumatized: first by the death of wild animals and then by the massive damage wrought on Australia's ecosystems. But while caring for others has been their top priority, zoo vets have also needed to attend to their own health, Vogelnest told me. "We are helping, we're saving these animals, we're doing our best to ensure good welfare outcomes. [But] when this all settles down, I suspect there'll be a few vets that will

Figure C.1 Larry Vogelnest, Senior Veterinarian at the Taronga Wildlife Hospital, cares for a burned koala at the Melbourne Zoo on January 2020. Courtesy of the Melbourne Zoo.

just fall ill. I mean, they'll basically be suffering." Care for the self is of utmost importance, he emphasized, insisting that it should not be neglected when caring for the health of our earth.

Reflecting on the coronavirus outbreak, veterinarian Sharon Deem of the Saint Louis Zoo highlighted a different form of neglect. According to Deem, many One Health proponents tend to overlook the ecological aspect in the One Health triad. She is wary of such tendencies to highlight the plight of humans and disregard everything else. And while she admitted that 75 percent of emerging infectious diseases in humans are zoonotic and originate principally from wildlife, she is concerned that "people often come back to wildlife as the bad guys." Walzer highlighted along these lines: "While zoonotic viruses are the most frequently-emerging human pathogen, they constitute less than 15 percent of all known species of human pathogens" (2018). Deem further reflected on this point in our January 2020 interview:

Most people have no idea that Ebola has wiped out half of the great apes in areas in the Congo. They just think of it as a human disease. So we jump right into our concern for humans. But in the long run, we are going to shoot ourselves in the foot because we are not going to get down to the root cause at the conservation level. The only positive thing in the Wuhan [incident] is that people are saying [that] we need to close down wet markets. [So] we are realizing that we need to figure out ways to feed humans—but not at the cost of wildlife trafficking and human pandemics.

"In a zoo vet book it would be really nice to bring out the bidirectional aspect of these problems," Deem offered. "In 50 years, we could be a planet of 11 billion people and billions of domestic animals, but close to zero free-living wild animal populations. How pathetic is that? . . . It's tragic." In 2019 (notably, before the outbreak of COVID-19), global leaders in wildlife management and human health drafted ten principles—referred to as the "Berlin Principles"—urgently calling for all sectors to mount a united effort to prevent the emergence or resurgence of diseases that threaten humans, wildlife, and livestock (Walzer, interview).

While most zoo vets do not work in wildlife rescue centers (like Vogelnest) or come up with policy proposals for managing the Wuhan coronavirus outbreak (like Walzer), this multidisciplinary way of thinking is arguably the direction in which the zoo veterinary profession is, and should be, heading. The new zoo veterinarian thus emerges as an epic figure who bears the burden of the tensions between wildlife management and the suffering bodies of individual animals, between healing and culling. This new zoo vet must care about and mourn not only the compromised life and premature death of individual animals in a wildfire or in a new disease outbreak, but also the dramatic demise of habitats and ecosystems that support the diversity of life on this planet.

At the same time, the figure of the new zoo veterinarian also brings hope, as she integrates multiple professional and disciplinary approaches and adapts to the complex interspecies challenges of this time. Caring for animals in the Anthropocene, this zoo vet must always recognize the limits of her own expertise as well as carefully consider those of others. Accordingly, a select group of zoo vets have become strong advocates of conservation medicine and One Health. My book has documented the "wilding" of the zoo veterinarian profession, and the fierce debates this diverse community has been engaged in about the nature, and the future, of their profession.

The One Health initiative has brought a range of disciplines to the table. Yet this inclusivity merely highlights the absence of the humanities and the social sciences from what might be the most important conversation of our time: how to heal our living planet. When I first contacted her, Sharon Deem was delighted that a social scientist was taking interest in One Health, and repeatedly told me how crucial such nonmedical perspectives have been for One Health's transdisciplinary framework. Without anthropologists, she said, we would not have understood local burial practices that have contributed to the spread of Ebola and could not have then effected change on this front. She hoped that this book might encourage further engagement by social scientists.

But the role of the social scientists in this context can, and should, be broader than identifying local human practices that contribute to diseases. Social scientists can provide a mirror for One Health proponents to reflect on themselves, to recognize the limits of their expertise, as integrative and transdisciplinary as it already is, and to consider other forms of knowledge that move beyond the scientific ones. Arguably, decisions about the life and death of living beings, their populations, and their ecosystems should not be left exclusively to experts. Instead, a transparent and inclusive discussion must take place about how to care for our interconnected life on this diseased planet.

Interviews

1. Adkesson, Michael. Veterinarian, Brookfield Zoo, Chicago. Telephone. March 15, 2016.
2. Anglister, Nili. Former veterinarian, Wildlife Hospital, Raman Gan Safari Park. In-person interview, Tel Aviv University, Israel. December 22, 2019.
3. Anonymous. Staff Veterinarian. In-person interview & observations. December 24, 2018.
4. Avni-Magen, Nili. Chief Veterinarian, Jerusalem Biblical Zoo, Israel. In-person interview and observations, Jerusalem, July 7, 2019; Telephone interviews, November 28, 2019; January 12, 2020.
5. Bakal, Robert. Director, Animal Health and Welfare, National Aquarium, Baltimore. In-person interview, Baltimore, MD. September 27, 2018.
6. Baylina, Núria. Curator and Head of Conservation, Oceanário de Lisboa. Telephone interview. November 12, 2018.
7. Ben-Dov, Dganit. Veterinarian and chief inspector for the Israeli Animal Welfare Act. In-person interview, Tel Aviv, Israel. December 20, 2019.
8. Bernardino, Rui. Veterinarian, Lisbon Zoo. In-person interview, Lisbon, Portugal. July 9, 2018.
9. Bertelsen, Mads Frost. Head zoo veterinarian, Copenhagen Zoo. Telephone interview. December 6, 2019.
10. Cabay, Chrissy. Director, Shedd Aquarium's Microbiome Project. In-person interview, Chicago, IL. December 3, 2018.
11. Clayton, Leigh. Vice President, Animal Care and Welfare, National Aquarium. In-person interview, Baltimore, MD. September 27, 2018.
12. Deem, Sharon. Director, Institute for Conservation Medicine & Director, WildCare Institute Center for Chelonian Conservation, Saint Louis Zoo. Telephone interview. January 28, 2020.
13. Dold, Chris. Chief Zoological Officer, Sea World. In-person interview and observations, SeaWorld Parks, Orlando, FL. October 10, 2019.

14. Gass, Scott. Director of Communications, SeaWorld. In-person interview and observations, SeaWorld Parks, Orlando, FL. October 10, 2019.
15. Haulena, Martin. Head Veterinarian, Vancouver Aquarium Marine Science Center. Skype interview. December 18, 2018.
16. Helmick, Kelly. Supervisory Medical Officer, Smithsonian Conservation Biology Institute; Former President, American Association of Zoo Veterinarians. Telephone interview. February 15, 2016.
17. Hilsenroth, Rob. Director, AAZV. Telephone interview. February 15, 2016.
18. Horowitz, Yigal. Director, Wild Life Hospital & Chief Veterinarian, Ramat Gan Safari Zoological Center. In-person interview and observations, Ramat Gan, Israel. December 25, 2019.
19. Innis, Charlie. Director of Animal Health, New England Aquarium. In-person interview, New England Aquarium, Boston MA. September 27, 2019.
20. Joblon, Melissa, Associate Veterinarian, New England Aquarium. In-person interview, New England Aquarium, Boston MA. September 27, 2019.
21. Jørgensen, Kasper. Team Leader, Animal Department, National Aquarium Denmark, Den Blå Planet. In-person interview, Copenhagen, Denmark. July 30, 2018.
22. Kaufman, Liz. Head Aquarium Veterinarian, Jerusalem Biblical Zoo. In-person interview and observations, Jerusalem, Israel. July 7, 2019.
23. LePage, Véronique. Associate Veterinarian, Ripley's Aquarium of Canada. In-person interview, Toronto, Canada. November 22, 2018.
24. Memarian, Iman. Former veterinarian, Tehran Zoo. Telephone. December 9, 2019.
25. Ochs, Andreas. Senior Veterinarian & Deputy Zoological Director, Zoological Garden Berlin. In-person interview and observations, Berlin, Germany. June 20, 2018.
26. Parsons, Ed. Director of Husbandry, Ripley's Aquarium of Canada. In-person interview, Toronto, Canada. November 22, 2018.
27. Pereira, Nuno Marques. Veterinarian, Oceanário de Lisboa. In-person interview, Lisbon, Portugal. July 10, 2018.
28. Perrin, Kathryn. Veterinarian, Center for Zoo and Wild Animal Health, Copenhagen Zoo. In-person interview, Copenhagen, Denmark. July 30, 2018.
29. Rally, Heather. Veterinarian, PETA Foundation. Telephone interview. December 20, 2018.
30. Staggs, Lydia. Senior Staff Veterinarian, SeaWorld. In-person interviews and observation, SeaWorld Parks, Orlando FL. October 10 & 11, 2019.
31. Sós, Endre. Lead Veterinarian, Budapest Zoo. Telephone interview. January 19, 2020.

32. Tlusty, Michael & Andy Rhyne. Director, Ocean Sustainability Science, the New England Aquarium & Research Scientist, New England Aquarium. In-person interviews, Boston, MA. May 11, 2016.
33. Van Bonn, Bill. Vice President of Animal Health, the Shedd Aquarium. In-person interview, Chicago, IL; December 3 & 4, 2018; e-mail communication, December 14, 2018.
34. Vielgrader, Hanna. Veterinarian, Vienna Zoo. In-person interview and observations, Vienna, Austria. June 26, 2019.
35. Vogelnest, Larry. Senior veterinarian, Taronga Wildlife Hospital, Sydney, Australia. Telephone interview. January 23, 2020.
36. Walzer, Chris. Wildlife veterinarian, Executive Director of Wildlife Health at the Wildlife Conservation Society & University Professor and Chair for Conservation Medicine at the University of Veterinary Medicine in Vienna, Austria. Skype interview. January 16, 2020.
37. Winders, Delcianna J. Vice President & Deputy General Counsel. Captive Animal Law Enforcement. PETA Foundation. Telephone interview. December 17, 2018.

References

AAZV. n.d. About Us. Retrieved from http://www.aazv.org/?page=840.
AAZV. 1998. Guidelines for Zoo and Aquarium Veterinary Medical Programs and Veterinary Hospitals. Retrieved from http://c.ymcdn.com/sites/www.aazv.org/resource/resmgr/imported/zoo_aquarium_vet_med_guidelines.pdf.
AAZV. 2009. Guidelines for Zoo and Aquarium Veterinary Medical Programs and Veterinary Hospitals, 5th ed. Retrieved from https://www.jstor.org/stable/41262606?seq=1.
AAZV. 2012. Bylaws and Strategic Plan (available upon request).
Abrell, Elan L. 2016. *Saving Animals: Everyday Practices of Care and Rescue in the US Animal Sanctuary Movement*. PhD thesis. City University of New York.
Aguirre, Alonso A. et al. 2002. *Conservation Medicine: Ecological Health in Practice*. New York: Oxford University Press.
Aguirre, Alonso A. Ostfeld, Richard and Daszak, Peter. 2012. *New Directions in Conservation Medicine: Applied Cases of Ecological Health*. New York: Oxford University Press.
Algae Barn. n.d. Is There Really a Difference Between Wild-Caught and Aquacultured Marine Aquarium Livestock? Blog. Retrieved from https://www.algaebarn.com/blog/captive-bred-fish/wild-caught-vs-aquacultured/.
Alper, Ty. 2008. Anesthetizing the Public Conscience: Lethal Injection and Animal Euthanasia. *Fordham Urban Law Journal* 35: 817–855.
Arluke, Arnold. 1988. Sacrificial Symbolism in Animal Experimentation: Object or Pet? *Anthrozoös* 2(2): 98–117.
AVMA. 2013. Guidelines for the Euthanasia of Animals. Retrieved from https://www.avma.org/KB/Policies/Documents/euthanasia.pdf.
AZA. n.d. Ocean Conservation. Retrieved from https://www.aza.org/ocean_conservation.
AZA. 2015. Annual Report on Conservation and Science: Highlights. Retrieved from https://www.aza.org/assets/2332/aza_arcshighlights_2015_web1.pdf.

AZA. 2017. Species Survival Plan Programs. Retrieved from https://www.aza.org/species-survival-plan-programs.

Balcombe, Jonathan. 2016. *What a Fish Knows: The Inner Lives of Our Underwater Cousins.* New York: Scientific American.

BBC. 2014. How Many Healthy Animals Do Zoos Put Down? By Hannah Barnes, February 27. Retrieved from https://www.bbc.com/news/magazine-26356099.

Bekoff, Marc. 2012. "Zoothanasia" Is Not Euthanasia: Words Matter. *Psychology Today.* Retrieved from http://www.psychologytoday.com/blog/animal-emotions/201208/zoothanasia-is-not-euthanasia-words-matter.

Bekoff, Marc. 2014. Killing Healthy Zoo Animals Is Wrong—And the Public Agrees. *National Geographic.* Retrieved from http://news.nationalgeographic.com/news/2014/03/140327-copenhagen-zoo-giraffes-lions-animals-deaths-science-world/.

Benson, Etienne. 2011. Animal Writes: Historiography, Disciplinarity, and the Animal Trace. In Kalof, Linda and Montgomery, Georgina M. (eds.). *Making Animal Meaning.* East Lansing: Michigan State University Press, pp. 3–16.

Berkovits, Annette Libeskind. 2017. *Confessions of an Accidental Zoo Curator.* Tenth Planet Press.

Bertelsen, Mads Frost. 2019. Issues Surrounding Surplus Animals in Zoos. In Miller, R. Eric, Lamberski, Nadine and Calle, Paul P. (eds.). *Fowler's Zoo and Wild Animal Medicine Current Therapy, Volume 9.* St. Louis: Elsevier, pp. 134–136.

Bourke, Joanna. 2014. *The Story of Pain: From Prayer to Painkillers.* Oxford: Oxford University Press.

Braverman, Irus. 2010. Zoo Registrars: A Bewildering Bureaucracy. *Duke Environmental Law & Policy Forum* 21(1): 165–206.

Braverman, Irus. 2012. *Zooland: The Institution of Captivity.* Stanford: Stanford University Press.

Braverman, Irus. 2014. Captive for Life: Conserving Extinct Species through Ex Situ Breeding. In Gruen, Lori (ed.). *The Ethics of Captivity.* New York: Oxford University Press, pp. 193–212.

Braverman, Irus. 2015. *Wild Life: The Institution of Nature.* Stanford: Stanford University Press.

Braverman, Irus. 2016. Anticipating Endangerment: The Biopolitics of Threatened Species Lists. *BioSocieties* 12(1): 132–157.

Braverman, Irus. 2017. Captive: Zoometric Operations in Gaza. *Public Culture* 29(1): 191–215.

Braverman, Irus. 2018a. Saving Species, One Individual at a Time: Zoo Veterinarians between Welfare and Conservation. *Humanimalia* 9(2): 1–27.

Braverman, Irus. 2018b. Law's Underdog: A Call for Nonhuman Legalities. *Annual Review of Law and Social Science* 14: 127–144.

Braverman, Irus. 2019a. Fish Encounters: Aquariums and Their Veterinarians in a Rapidly Changing World. *Humanimalia* 11(1): 1–29.

Braverman, Irus. 2019b. Corals in the City: Cultivating Ocean Life in the Anthropocene Tank. *Contemporary Social Science: Journal of the Academy of Social Sciences* (Special Issue: Urban Animals: Cartographies of Radical Encounters). doi: 10.1080/21582041.2019.1688382.

Braverman, Irus. 2020. Fleshy Encounters: Meddling in the Lifeworlds of Zoo and Aquarium Veterinarians. *Humanimalia* 11(2): 49–75.

Butler, Judith. 2004. *Precarious Life: The Powers of Mourning and Violence.* New York: Verso.

Callicott, J. Baird. 1980. Animal Liberation: A Triangular Affair. *Environmental Ethics* 2: 311–328.

Canidae. 2014. A Quick History of Veterinary Medicine. By Linda Cole. Retrieved from https://www.canidae.com/blog/2014/11/a-quick-history-of-veterinary-medicine/.

CNN. 2014. Zoo Official on Marius the Giraffe: Conservation Isn't Always Clean. McLaughlin, E. and Wilkinson, P., February 10. Retrieved from http://www.cnn.com/2014/02/10/world/europe/denmark-zoo-giraffe/.

Coole, Diana and Samantha Frost. 2010. Introducing the New Materialisms. In Coole, Diana and Frost, Samantha (eds.). *New Materialisms: Ontology, Agency and Politics*. Durham: Duke University Press, pp. 1–46.

Deckha, Maneesha. 2013. Initiating a Non-Anthropocentric Jurisprudence: The Rule of Law and Animal Vulnerability under a Property Paradigm. *Alberta Law Review* 50(4): 783–814.

Deem, Sharon L. 2007. Role of the Zoo Veterinarian in the Conservation of Captive and Free-Ranging Wildlife. *International Zoo Yearbook* 41(1): 3–11.

Deem, Sharon L. 2018. *Conservation Medicine to One Health: The Role of Zoologic Veterinarians*. In Miller, Eric R. and Fo, Murray E. (eds.). *Fowler's Zoo and Wild Animal Medicine Current Therapy, Volume 8*. Saint Louis: Elsevier, pp. 698–702.

Deem, Sharon L., Lane-deGraaf, Kelly E., and Rayhel, Elizabeth A. 2019. *Introduction to One Health: An Interdisciplinary Approach to Planetary Health*. Hoboken: Wiley-Blackwell.

Despret, Vinciane. 2016. *What Would Animals Say If We Asked the Right Questions?* Minneapolis: University of Minnesota Press.

The Dodo. 2016. Finally: Aquarium Will No Longer Capture Dolphins and Whales from the Wild. Retrieved from https://www.thedodo.com/georgia-aquarium-stops-catching-wild-marine-mammals-1877822888.html.

Dror, Otniel E. 1999. The Affect of Experiment: The Turn to Emotions in Anglo-American Physiology, 1900–1940. *Isis* 90(2): 205–237.

EAZA. 2011. Policy Statement on Euthanasia. Approved by EAZA Council, September 26. Retrieved from EAZA. 2015. Culling Statement. Approved by EAZA Council, April 30. Retrieved from https://www.eaza.net/assets/Uploads/Position-statements/EAZA-Culling-statement.pdf.

EAZA. 2019. Standards for the Accommodation and Care of Animals in Zoos and Aquaria. Approved by EAZA Annual General Meeting, April 25. Retrieved from https://www.eaza.net/assets/Uploads/Standards-and-policies/2019-04-EAZA-Standards-for-Accomodation-and-Care.pdf.

EAZA Biobank. n.d. Retrieved from https://www.eaza.net/conservation/research/eaza-biobank/.

Encyclopedia Britannica. n.d. Aquariums. Retrieved from https://www.britannica.com/science/aquarium.

FishBase. 2018. Retrieved from https://www.fishbase.us/.

Föllmi, Jérôme et al. 2007. A Scoring System to Evaluate Physical Condition and Quality of Life in Geriatric Zoo Mammals. *Animal Welfare* 16: 309–318.

Fowler, Murray E. 2006. *A History of the American Association of Zoo Veterinarians*. Yulee, Florida: American Association of Zoo Veterinarians.

Grassmann, Michael, McNeil, Bryan, and Warton, Jim. 2017. Sharks in Captivity: The Role of Husbandry, Breeding, Education, and Citizen Science in Shark Conservation. *Advances in Marine Biology* 78: 89–119.

Grazian, David. 2015. *American Zoo: A Sociological Safari*. Princeton, NJ: Princeton University Press.

The Guardian. 2014. Marius the Giraffe Killed at Copenhagen Zoo Despite Worldwide Protests. Eriksen, Lars and Kennedy, Maev. February 9, Retrieved from https://www.theguardian.com/world/2014/feb/09/marius-giraffe-killed-copenhagen-zoo-protests.

Gunther, Mark. 2018. Fish Are Getting Their Animal Rights Moment. *Civil Eats*, January 18. Retrieved from https://civileats.com/2018/01/18/fish-are-getting-their-animal-rights-moment/.

Haraway, Donna. 2003. *The Companion Species Manifesto: Dogs, People, and Significant Others*. Chicago: Prickly Paradigm.

Haraway, Donna. 2008. *When Species Meet*. Minneapolis: University of Minnesota Press.

Heath, Christian, Luff, Paul, Sanchez-Svensson, Marcus and Nicholls, Maxim. 2018. Exchanging Implements: The Micro-Materialities of Multidisciplinary Work in the Operating Theatre. *Sociology of Health & Illness* 40: 297–313.

Holmberg, Tora. 2011. Mortal Love: Care Practices in Animal Experimentation. *Feminist Theory* 12(2): 147–163.

Holst, Bengt. 2014. Euthanasia of a 2 Year Old Male Giraffe at Copenhagen Zoo. Retrieved from http://www.zoo.dk/files/2014_Giraffe_case-explanation_15_MAY.pdf.

Humane Endpoints. n.d. Retrieved from https://www.humane-endpoints.info/en.

Hurn, Samantha and Alexander Badman-King. 2019. Care as an Alternative to Euthanasia? Reconceptualizing Veterinary Palliative and End-of-life Care. *Medical Anthropology Quarterly* 33: 138–155.

Jasanoff, Sheila. 1996. *Science at the Bar: Law, Science, and Technology in America*. Cambridge: Harvard University Press.

Jones, Susan D. 2003. *Valuing Animals: Veterinarians and their Patients in Modern America*. Baltimore: The Johns Hopkins University Press.

Junger, Ernst. [1957] 2000. *The Glass Bees*. New York: New York Review Book.

Karesh, William B. 1995. Wildlife Rehabilitation: Additional Considerations for Developing Countries. *Journal of Zoo and Wildlife Medicine* 26(1): 2–9.

Kelly, Paul, Stack, David and Harley, Jessica. 2013. A Review of the Proposed Reintroduction Program for the Far Eastern Leopard (*Panthera pardus orientalis*) and the Role of Conservation Organizations, Veterinarians, and Zoos. *Topics in Companion Animal Medicine* 28: 163–166.

Key, Brian. 2016. Why Fish Do Not Feel Pain. *Animal Sentience* 3. Retrieved from https://animalstudiesrepository.org/cgi/viewcontent.cgi?referer=&httpsredir=1&article=1011&context=animsent.

Khan, Laura. 2017. Meat, Monkey, and Mosquitoes. YouTube. December 14. Retrieved from https://www.youtube.com/watch?v=ITELu0TdJZA.

King, Lonnie J. et al. 2008. One Health Initiative Task Force Report. *Journal of the American Veterinary Medical Association* 233(2): 259–261.

Latour, Bruno. 2005. *Reassembling the Social: An Introduction to Actor-Network-Theory*. Oxford: Oxford University Press.

Latour, Bruno. 2009. *The Making of Law: An Ethnography of the Conseil d'Etat*. Cambridge: Polity

Law, John. 2010. Care and Killing: Tensions in Veterinary Practice. In Mol, Annemarie, Moser, Ingunn and Pols, Jeannette (eds.). *Care in Practice*. Berlin: Transcript Verlag, pp. 57–72.

Lerner, Henrik and Berg, Charlotte. 2017. A Comparison of Three Holistic Approaches to Health: One Health, EcoHealth, and Planetary Health. *Frontiers in Veterinary Science* 4(163): 1–7.

MacGregor, Hayley and Waldman, Linda. 2017. Views from Many Worlds: Unsettling Categories in Interdisciplinary Research on Endemic Zoonotic Diseases. *Philosophical Transactions of the Royal Society B* 372 (1725): 20160170. doi:10.1098/rstb.2016.0170.

Maller, Cecily Jane. 2015. Understanding Health through Social Practices: Performance and Materiality in Everyday Life. *Sociology of Health & Illness* 37(1): 52–66.

Margulis, Lynn and Fester, René (eds.). 1991. *Symbiosis as a Source of Evolutionary Innovation Speciation and Morphogenesis*. Cambridge: MIT Press.

Marx, Vivien. 2015. PCR Heads into the Field. *Nature Methods* 12(5): 393–397.

McCulloch, Steven P. and Reiss, Michael J. 2016. Marius the Giraffe and Euthanasia of Zoo Animals. In Mullan, Siobhan and Fawcett, Anne (eds.). *Veterinary Ethics: Navigating Tough Cases*. Sheffield: 5m Publishing.
McMahan, Jeff. 2002. *The Ethics of Killing: Problems at the Margin*. Oxford: Oxford University Press.
Midgley, Mary. [1978] 2005. *Beast and Man: The Roots of Human Nature*. London: Routledge.
Minteer, Ben and Collins, James. 2013. Ecological Ethics in Captivity: Balancing Values and Responsibilities in Zoo and Aquarium Research under Rapid Global Change. *Institute for Laboratory Animal Research Journal* 54(1): 41–51.
Mol, Annemarie. 2002. *The Body Multiple: Ontology in Medical Practice*. Durham: Duke University Press.
Mol, Annemarie, Moser, Ingunn and Pols, Jeannette (eds.). 2010. *Care in Practice: On Tinkering in Clinics, Homes and Farms*. Bielefeld, Germany: Transcript Publishers.
Montgomery, Sy. 2015. *The Soul of an Octopus: A Surprising Exploration into the Wonder of Consciousness*. New York: Astria.
Moore, R.S., and Nekaris K.A.I. 2014. Compassionate Conservation, Rehabilitation and Translocation of Indonesian Slow Lorises. *Endangered Species Research* 26(2): 93–102.
Morris. Patricia. 2012. *Blue Juice: Euthanasia in Veterinary Medicine*. Philadelphia: Temple University Press.
Moscoso, Javier. 2012. *Pain: A Cultural History*. New York: Palgrave Macmillan.
Moses, Lisa, Malowney, Monia J. and Wesley Boyd, Jon. 2018. Ethical Conflict and Moral Distress in Veterinary Practice: A Survey of North American Veterinarians. *Journal of Veterinary Internal Medicine* 32: 2115–2122.
National Geographic. 2014. Killing of Marius the Giraffe Exposes Myths about Zoos. Morell, Virginia, February 13. Retrieved from http://news.nationalgeographic.com/news/2014/02/140212-giraffe-death-denmark-copenhagen-zoo-breeding-europe/.
The New Yorker. 2017. Killing Animals at the Zoo. Parker, Ian, January 10. Retrieved from http://www.newyorker.com/magazine/2017/01/16/killing-animals-at-the-zoo.
Norris, Scott. 2001. A New Voice in Conservation: Conservation Medicine Seeks to Bring Ecologists, Veterinarians, and Doctors Together Around a Simple Unifying Concept: Health. *BioScience* 51(1): 7–12.
Oreskes, Naomi. 2019. *Why Trust Science?* Princeton: Princeton University Press.
Palmer, Clare Alexandra. 2006. Killing Animals in Animal Shelters. In Animal Studies Group (ed.). *Killing Animals*. Champaign: University of Illinois Press, pp. 170–187.

Palmer, Clare Alexandra. 2018. Kill, Incarcerate, or Liberate? Ethics and Alternatives to Orangutan Rehabilitation. *Biological Conservation* 227: 181–188.

Paquet, Paul C. and Darimont, Chris T. 2010. Wildlife Conservation and Animal Welfare: Two Sides of the Same Coin? *Animal Welfare* 19: 177–90.

PBS. 2015. Why Can't Captive Breeding of Saltwater Aquarium Fish Catch On? February 15. Retrieved from https://www.pbs.org/newshour/nation/cant-captive-breeding-saltwater-aquarium-fish-catch-2.

Pierce, Jessica. 2016. *Run Spot Run: The Ethics of Keeping Pets.* Chicago: University of Chicago Press.

RCVS Knowledge. n.d. Retrieved from https://knowledge.rcvs.org.uk/heritage-and-history/history-of-the-veterinary-profession/.

Rhoades, Rebecca H. 2002. *The Humane Society of the United States: Euthanasia Training Manual* 43. Retrieved from https://www.animalsheltering.org/sites/default/files/documents/euthanasia-reference-manual.pdf.

Ridgway, Sam H. 2008. History of Veterinary Medicine and Marine Mammals: A Personal Perspective. *Aquatic Mammals* 34(4): 471–513.

Ridgway, Sam H., Kenneth, Norris S. and Cornell, Lanny H. 1989. Some Considerations for Those Wishing to Propagate Platanistoid Dolphins. In Perrin, William F., Borwnell Jr., Robert L., Zhou, Kaiya and Liu, Jiankang (eds.). *Biology and Conservation of River Dolphins.* Gland: IUCN Species Survival Commission Occasional Papers (no. 3), pp. 159–167.

Ripley's Aquarium. Life Support Systems. Retrieved from https://www.ripleyaquariums.com/canada/galleries/life-support-systems/.

Ritvo, Harriet. 2007. On the Animal Turn. *Daedalus* 136: 118–122.

Rose, J. D. et al. 2014. Can Fish Really Feel Pain? *Fish and Fisheries* 15(1): 97–133.

Roy, Deboleena. 2012. Cosmopolitics and the Brain. In *Neurofeminism.* London: Palgrave-Macmillan, pp. 175–192.

Safina, Carl. 2018. Are We Wrong to Assume Fish Can't Feel Pain? *The Guardian*, October 30. Retrieved from https://www.theguardian.com/news/2018/oct/30/are-we-wrong-to-assume-fish-cant-feel-pain.

Sanders, Clinton R. 2010. Working Out Back: The Veterinary Technician and "Dirty Work." *Journal of Contemporary Ethnography* 39(3): 243–272.

SEAZA. n.d. Constitution, pp. 47–61. Retrieved from http://www.zooreach.org/ZooLegislation/Zoo%20legislation%20SEA.pdf.

Selzer, Richard. [1974] 1996. *Mortal Lessons: Notes on the Art of Surgery.* San Diego: Harcourt Brace & Company.

Shmuely, Shira. 2019. Curare: The Poisoned Arrow That Entered the Laboratory and Sparked a Moral Debate. *Social History of Medicine* hky124: 1–17.

Shukin, Nichole. 2009. *Animal Capital: Rendering Life in Biopolitical Times.* Minneapolis: University of Minnesota Press.

Slate. 2017. How Does an Aquarium Veterinarian Work? By Jacob Brogan, May 22. Retrieved from http://www.slate.com/articles/podcasts/working/2017/05/how_does_leigh_clayton_the_national_aquarium_s_director_of_animal_health.html.

Spelman, Lucy H. and Ted Y. Mashima (eds.). 2008. *The Rhino with Glue-On Shoes: And Other Surprising Stories of Zoo Vets and Their Patients*. New York: Delacorte Press.

Stengers, Isabelle (Penelope Deutscher, trans.). 2000. Another Look: Relearning to Laugh. *Hypatia* 15(4): 41–54.

Stengers, Isabelle. 2005. Introductory Note on an Ecology of Practices. *Cultural Studies Review* 11(1): 183–196.

Stengers, Isabelle. 2010. *Cosmopolitics: Vol. I*. Minneapolis: University of Minnesota Press.

Stokstad, Eric. 2013. New Hope for an Endangered Fish in Madagascar. *Science Magazine*, December 13. Retrieved from https://www.sciencemag.org/news/2013/12/new-hope-endangered-fish-madagascar.

Tallis, Raymond. 2003. *The Hand: A Philosophical Inquiry into Human Beings*. Edinburgh: Edinburgh University Press.

Tomasi, S.E. et al. 2019. Suicide among Veterinarians in the United States from 1979 through 2015. *Journal of the American Veterinary Medical Association* 254(1): 104–112.

Tsing, Anna. 2012. Unruly Edges: Mushrooms as Companion Species. *Environmental Humanities* 1: 141–154.

USDA. n.d. Humane Endpoints and Euthanasia. Retrieved from https://www.nal.usda.gov/awic/humane-endpoints-and-euthanasia.

VAG. 2001. Guidelines for Veterinary Advisor Group. Retrieved from http://www.aazv.org/?331.

The Veterinary Student. 1939. History of Veterinary Medicine. *Iowa State University Veterinarian* 2(1): 6–10. Retrieved from http://lib.dr.iastate.edu/iowastate_veterinarian/vol2/iss1/1.

Vitali, S., Reiss, A. and Eden, P. 2011. Conservation Medicine in and through Zoos. *International Zoo Yearbook* 45: 160–167.

Vogelnest, Larry and Jessica J. Talbot. 2019. Quality-of-Life Assessment and End-of-Life Planning for Geriatric Zoo Animals. In Miller, R. Eric, Lamberski, Nadine and Calle, Paul P. (eds.). *Fowler's Zoo and Wild Animal Medicine Current Therapy, Volume 9*. St. Louis: Elsevier, pp. 83–91.

Wailoo, Keith. 2014. *Pain: A Political History*. Baltimore: The Johns Hopkins University Press.

Walzer, Chris. 2017. Beyond One Health—Zoological Medicine in the Anthropocene. *Frontiers in Veterinary Science* 4(102): 1–3. doi:10.3389/fvets.2017.00102.

Weber, Sam. 2015. Why Can't Captive Breeding of Saltwater Aquarium Fish Catch On? *PBS*. February 15. Retrieved from https://www.pbs.org/newshour/nation/cant-captive-breeding-saltwater-aquarium-fish-catch-2.

West, Annie G. et al. 2019. The Microbiome in Threatened Species Conservation. *Biological Conservation* 229: 85–98.

Wilbert, Chris. 2006. Killing Animals: An Introduction. In Wilbert, Chris (ed.). *Killing Animals*. Champaign: The University of Illinois Press.

Wilkinson, Lise. 1992. *Animals and Disease*. Cambridge: Cambridge University Press.

Wolfe, Cary. 2012. *Before the Law: Humans and Other Animals in a Biopolitical Frame*. Chicago: University of Chicago Press.

Woodford, Michael H. (ed.). 2000. *Quarantine and Health Screening Protocols for Wildlife Prior to Translocation and Release into the Wild*. IUCN Veterinary Specialist Group, OIE, Care for the Wild, UK, and the European Association of Wildlife Veterinarians, Switzerland.

Woods, Abigail, Bresalier, Michael, Cassidy, Angela, and Mason Dentinger, Rachel. 2018. *Animals and the Shaping of Modern Medicine: One Health and its Histories*. Cham: Palgrave-Macmillan.

Yanong, Roy P.E. et al. 2007. Fish Slaughter, Killing, and Euthanasia: A Review of Major Published U.S. Guidance Documents and General Considerations of Methods. University of Florida IFAS.

ZAAA. 2015. Zoo and Aquarium Association Australasia: Guidelines— Animal Euthanasia. Approved by the Board of the Association, October 10. Retrieved from https://zooaquarium.org.au/common/Uploaded%20 files/Portal/Policies/1b_2_G_Euthanasia.pdf.

ZSL. n.d. The History of the Aquarium. Retrieved from https://www.zsl. org/zsl-london-zoo/exhibits/the-history-of-the-aquarium.

Index

AAZV *see* Association of Zoo Veterinarians (AAZV)
Adkesson, Michael 23–25, 34–36
Agamben, Giorgio 117
Alper, Ty 88
American Association of Zoos and Aquariums (AZA) 22, 30, 49; 2015 Annual Report on Conservation Science 34
American Association of Zoo Veterinarians (AAZV) 20–21, 29; Guidelines 30; Article 2(e) 21
American Medical Association 12
American Veterinary Association (AVA) 12
Amling Jr., H. 20
Animal Capital (Nicole Shukin) 117
animal categories 117, 125, 126; domestic/captive/wild 14–15, 31; lab 12, 120; species-based 11, 13; *see also* biopolitics; captive animals; domestic/farm animals; human–animal divide/distinction/boundaries
animal rights 45, 79, 85, 94, 104, 123
animal traces/agency 11, 14–16, 20, 49, 66, 70, 71, 120
animal turn 11, 13
Animal Veterinary Medicine Association (AVMA): 2013 Guidelines for the Euthanasia of Animals 85, 118–121
animal welfare 2, 12, 29, 30, 32, 37, 62, 68, 83, 86, 88, 96, 120, 123, 124; *vs.* animal rights 45, 79, 85, 94, 104, 123; and conservation 17–44, 104, 113; hierarchies in 30–33; *see also* euthanasia, animal; pain/suffering, animal
Animal Welfare Act of 1966, 21, 120
"Animal Welfare and Conservation: An Essential Connection" (Paul Waldau) 123
aquaculture 45
aquariums 45–62; bacteria in 9, 67; fish capture for 56–57; future of 62; history of 46–49; observation as scientific knowledge in 49–52; fish pain in 60–62; *vs.* pet and ornamental industries 55; water environment in 46, 63–68
Aristotle 19
Art of Surgery, The (Richard Selzer) 80–81
Association of Veterinary Medicine 20
Australian wildlife 2, 40, 61, 108, 127, 131, 132
AVA *see* American Veterinary Association (AVA)
AVMA *see* Animal Veterinary Medicine Association (AVMA)
Avni-Magen, Nili 79, 89, 93, 94, 101, 112, 114, 115

AZA *see* American Association of Zoos and Aquariums (AZA)

bacteria 43, 50–52, 56–57, 82; aquarium-dwelling 9, 67; enterococci 67; filamentous bacteria 67; in Micropia 9; as "patients" 66; *see also* holobiont; microbiome
Bakal, Robert 49–50
Balcombe, Jonathan 61
Baltimore National Aquarium 58
bats, fruit 114–115
Baylina, Núria 48–49, 57–58, 63
Beast and Man (Mary Midgley) 80
Before the Law: Humans and Other Animals in a Biopolitical Frame (Cary Wolfe) 117
Bekoff, Marc 87, 123
Berlin Principles 134
Berlin Zoo 63
Bernardino, Rui 65
Bertelsen, Mads 18, 90–93, 96, 107, 110–118, 127
biobank 114
biopolitics 19, 33, 44; in animal management 32; hierarchies 33; and violence 117
biosafety 42
Blue Juice: Euthanasia in Veterinary Medicine (Patricia Morris) 87
body multiple 82
Bourgelat, Claude 20
"breed and cull" 10, 113, 121; *see also* euthanasia, animal
breeding 22, 30, 80, 87, 93, 109, 110; captive 1, 14, 15, 17, 28, 41, 42, 55–57, 59, 114; collaborative program 22, 57, 89, 114; inbreeding 29, 59
Budapest Zoo 101, 112
Butler, Judith 100

Cabay, Chrissy 66–67
captive animals 13, 21–22, 30, 34, 39, 41, 57, 58–59, 82, 107; *see also* animal categories
captive breeding 1, 14, 15, 17, 28, 41, 42, 55–57, 59, 114
care/caring 84–122; for animals 1, 2, 22–28, 78, 95, 134; four objects of 122; for oneself 121–122, 132–133; triaging 131–135
CBSG *see* Conservation Breeding Specialist Group (CBSG)
Centers for Disease Control 12, 40
Chicago Zoological Society: WelfareTrak® 95
Clayton, Leigh 23, 26, 50, 52–53
climate change/global warming 1, 2, 13, 46, 59, 123, 125, 132
clinical gaze (outlook) 75–79
Collins, James 30, 41
compassionate conservation 124
compassion fatigue 121–122
conservation 8, 9, 77, 87, 89, 92, 97, 112, 114; in aquariums 45, 46, 53, 54, 57–60, 62; and biodiversity 13; compassionate 123–124; ecosystem 19; management 68, 104, 113; medicine 2, 12–13, 40, 41, 60, 83, 94, 118, 124–126, 130, 134; science beyond 67; *in situ—ex situ* 1, 19, 22, 30, 33, 34, 38, 43, 83, 85, 86, 99, 101, 104, 106, 107, 109, 121; welfare and 17–44, 104, 113; and "wildlife welfare" ethic 124
Conservation Breeding Specialist Group (CBSG): One Plan 13
Conservation Medicine: Ecological Health in Practice (Aguirre) 12
contraception 28, 89, 108, 112
Copenhagen Zoo 17, 28, 30, 31, 55, 58, 60, 87, 90, 110, 113–115, 117, 127
co-production 11, 14, 70
cosmopolitics 3
COVID-19/coronavirus 2, 131, 133, 134; *see also* zoonotic diseases
crane, sandhill 99–100, 102, 104
cross/inter-disciplinary 8, 16, 124, 126
culling 30, 84, 87, 110–115, 121, 134; *see also* euthanasia, animal

Darimont, Chris 124
database, animal 33, 40, 95

Deckha, Maneesha 13
Deem, Sharon 34, 104, 133–134, 135
deer: white-tailed 32–33, fallow 94, *115*
Denmark National Aquarium 57, 66, 81
Despret, Vinciane 84, 100, 114
Dickie, Lesley 109
diseased planet 2, 125, 131, 135
Dold, Chris 72, 75–77
dolphins 47, 50, 58, 67, 72, 77, 82, 103, 105–106
domestic/farm animals 13, 14, 26, 27, 30–31, 41, 68, 83, 125, 134; in aquariums 52; cats 5, 26, 49, 50, 76, 88, 93, 94, 100, 112, 129; cows 49, 51, 77, 116, 129, 130; dogs 19, 26, 47, 49, 50, 72, 76, 88, 94; euthanasia and 96; horses 19, 26, 94; *see also* animal categories

Earle, Sylvia 61
EAZA *see* European Association of Zoos and Aquariums (EAZA)
Ebola 134, 135; *see also* zoonotic diseases
EcoHealth 13, 118; *see also* One Health
ecology of practices 3
EEP *see* European Endangered Species Programme (EEP)
Endangered Species Act 34
epidemiology 82, 83, 124–125
European Association of Zoos and Aquariums (EAZA) 114; biobank 114; Euthanasia Statement 86; Article 2, 86; Article 4, 86; 2014 Standards for the Accommodation and Care of Animals in Zoos and Aquaria 109–110
European Convention for the Protection of Vertebrate Animals used for Experimental and other Scientific Purposes: Article 5, 120; Article 11, 120
European Endangered Species Programme (EEP) 17, 22, 114

euthanasia, animal 2, 10, 14, 18, 30, 84–122; and assisted killing 88; of bats 114–115; and "breed and cull" 10, 113, 121; of crane 99–100; culture of 85; of fish 118–121; of healthy zoo animals 109–118; in humans *vs*. nonhumans 87–88; of lions 111–114; of Marius the giraffe 17–18, 28–29, 30, 31, 80, 85, 86, 87, 90, 116, 117; medical *vs*. non-medical 88–99; and the "preponderance of the accumulated evidence" principle 118–119; regulatory patchwork for 118–121; zoo *vs*. non-zoo animals 99–109; *see also* animal welfare; killing (animals)

fish: capture of wild 56; euthanizing 118–121; pain 60–62; *see also* aquariums
Fish and Wildlife Service, United States 31
Föllmi, Jérôme 95
Foucault, Michel 117

Gass, Scott 103–104
genetic diversity 29, 59
Gosse, Philip Henry 46–47
governing: animals 15, 86; death/killing 14, 121
grievable life 100, 117

hand *see* tools
Haraway, Donna 84
healthy zoo animals, euthanasia for 109–118
Heath, Christian 71
Helmick, Kelly 28, 21, 22, 27, 29–33, 38, 39, 42
Hilsenroth, Rob 21, 29, 33, 35
Hippocrates 19
holobiont 43
Holst, Bengt 17
Horowitz, Yigal 72, 92–93, 101
human–animal divide/distinction/boundaries 3, 20, 40, 88, 127–131; *see also* animal categories

human–animal lifeworlds 11–14
humane endpoint 120
husbandry 2, 14, 21, 38, 59

ibex, Nubian 72–73
Ignoring Nature No More: The Case for Compassionate Conservation (Marc Bekoff) 123
inbreeding 29, 59
in situ—*ex situ* 1, 19, 22, 30, 33, 35, 38, 39, 43, 83, 85, 86, 99, 107, 109, 121
instruments *see* tools
insurance populations 22
intensive population management 32
International Association of Aquatic Animal Medicine 46, 47
Israel Aquarium, Jerusalem 49
invertebrates 49–50, 120, 131; pain in 60

Jerusalem Zoo 79, 88, 93, 101, 112, 115
Joblon, Melissa 81–82, 104–107
Jørgensen, Kasper 50–51, 55–56, 58–60

Kant, Immanuel 3
Key, Brian 61
killing (animals) 17–19, 28–30, 84–122; *see also* euthanasia, animal
Killing Animals (Chris Wilbert) 84–85
koala 108–109, 132, *133*
Kosch, Philip 40

lab 9, 14, 83, 98; animals 13, 120; testing 72; zoo as 90; *see also* animal categories
Latour, Bruno 128
law (legalities) 29, 55, 87; and the animal turn 11, 13; animal welfare 120; as anthropocentric 13; bylaws 21; guidelines 2, 15, 21–22, 85, 86, 106, 118–119, 120; outside of 14; Sharia 96; soft 14
Law, John 78, 122

LePage, Véronique 51, 62, 120
lifeworlds 2, 11–14, 82, 114
lion(s): and euthanasia 111–112, 113–114; thinking like a 114
Lisbon Oceanarium 47, 48, 50, 57, 118
Lisbon Zoo 53, 58, 63–65, 69
lizard 26, 49; frilled neck 4–7, 78, 96, 127, 129, 130
London Zoological Society 46, 47
Lovejoy, Thomas 12–13
Lovvorn, Jonathan 123

MacGregor, Hayley 126
McNamara, Tracey 40
marine animals, reintroducing 58–60
Marius (the giraffe) 17–18, 28–29, 30, 31, 80, 85, 86, 87, 90, 116, 117; *see also* euthanasia, of healthy zoo animals
materialities 63
meddling 1–16, 83, 131
medical humanities 11–12, 13, 131
medical posthumanities 11, 117, 127
Memarian, Iman 96–98, 127
microbiome 66, 68, 124
Midgley, Mary 80
Minteer, Ben 30, 41
Mol, Annemarie 123, 131
more-than-human legalities 13, 14
Morris, Patricia 87
multiplicity 50, 126
multispecies 13, 118; ethnography 11

Neal, Leah 55
neuromuscular blocking agents 88
New Directions in Conservation Medicine (Lovejoy) 12–13
New England Aquarium 54, 81, 104
new zoo veterinarian 83, 123–127, 134; *see also* One Health
Noah's Ark 59

One Health 2, 118; *vs.* compassionate conservation 123–125; criticism toward 126–127, 133–135; definition

and history 12–13, 41, 130; epidemiology 82, 83, 124–125; and inter/multi/tri-disciplinarity 12–16, 41, 82, 125, 135; and law/legal experts 14, 16; and the medical posthumanities 117, 130; social science/humanities contribution to 12, 16, 117, 126–127, 135; *see also* EcoHealth; One Medicine
One Medicine 12
orcas 58, 90, *91*, 127
organoleptic 72
Ostfeld, Richard 124–125
otter 59, 89–90, 95, 100–101

pain/suffering, animal 5, 26, 58, 60–62, 72, 78, 85–90, 93, 94, 96–99, 102, 104, 105, 107, 118–121, 127, 132; in captivity 58; definition of 85; and extinction 58; and humane endpoint 120; nociceptive reflex *vs.* cognitive 60; *see also* euthanasia, animal; killing (animals)
pathogens 38, 40, 43, 59, 83, 118, 133; pathogen packages 38, 118
Papyrus, Kahun 19
Paquet, Paul 124
PCR *see* polymerase chain reaction (PCR)
penguins 23, 34, *35*, 58
Pereira, Nuno 47–48, 50, 118
Perrin, Kathryn 55–56, 60, 61–62
Persian leopard 97, *98*
Pierce, Jessica 88
planetary health 13
planet doctors 123–135
pollution 46, 58, 59
polymerase chain reaction (PCR) 83, 125
posthumanities/posthumanism 11, 12, 117, 126, 127, 131
puffer fish, cross river 74–75, 76

Quarantine and Health Screening Protocols for Wildlife Prior to Translocation and Release into the Wild (Michael Woodford) 43

Ramat Gan Safari Zoological Center 72–73, 92–93, 101
regulatory: patchwork 118–120; practices 8, 43, 121; regimes 13, 21, 55, 87
rehabilitation 1, 32, 37, 75, 85, 97, 104, 107, 108, 110
reintroductions 1, 22, 24, 33, 41–43, 93, 115, 128; of marine animals 58–60
reproduction 28; *see also* breeding
rescue centers 35–37, 86, 101, 132, 134
restoration 41
Rhyne, Andy 54
Ridgway, Sam 47
Ripley's Aquarium, Toronto, Canada 51, 55, 62, 65, 120
Rose, James 60–61
Roy, Deboleena 3

SAFE: Saving Animals from Extinction 58
safety 26–27, 37, 86, 119
Saint Louis Zoo 104, 133
San Diego Zoo 114
schooling fish *vs.* individual fish 51–52
Science and Technology Studies (STS) 11, 78, 84, 122, 128
scientific knowledge 33, 38, 49–52
scissors *see* tools
Scripps Institution of Oceanography 47
sea lions 34, *36*, *53*, 103
SeaWorld Park, Orlando, Florida 63, 64, 72, 75, 76, 89–90, 95, 99, 102, 103, 129
SEAZA *see* South East Asian Zoo Association (SEAZA)
Selzer, Richard 79, 80–81
Sharia law 96
shark 51, 52, 56–57, 58, 61, 67, 106
Shedd Aquarium, Chicago 58, 63, 66–67, 71, 79; Microbiome Project in 67
Shukin, Nicole 117
sight (e.g., of animals' inner organs) 73, 80, 81, 100

Sós, Endre 36–39, 101–102, 112–113
South East Asian Zoo Association (SEAZA) 87
spaces: aquarium 46, 63–66; veterinary 2, 15, 63–71; zoo 17, 22, 37, 89, 90, 96, 111
Species Survival Plans (SSPs) 22
Spooner, Charles 20
SSPs *see* Species Survival Plans (SSPs)
Staggs, Lydia 69–70, 89–91, 95, 99–104
Stengers, Isabelle 3–4
stingrays 57, 67, *81*
STS *see* Science and Technology Studies (STS)
studbooks 22, 57
surgery 4–6, 21, 68, 71, 74, 75, 79–82, 96

T-61 5, *98*
Talbot, Jessica J. 95
Tallis, Raymond 70
Taronga Zoo, Sydney 99, 108, 122, 132
Taxon Advisory Groups 21
technologies 68–71
Tehran Zoo 96, 127
Tlusty, Michael 54
tools 68–71; hands as 70–71; scissors as 2, 6, 68–71, 82, 125
Tsing, Anna 126
turtles, sea 58, 67; "de-oiling" of 102; stranded 102–103, 104

United States Department of Agriculture (USDA) 120
USDA *see* United States Department of Agriculture (USDA)

VAG *see* Veterinary Advisory Group (VAG)
Van Bonn, Bill 9, 66, 67, 71, 73–75, 80, 82

VA *see* Veterinary Advisor (VA)
Vegetius 19–20
Veterinary Advisor (VA) 22
Veterinary Advisory Group (VAG) 22
veterinary spaces *see* spaces, veterinary
"Views from Many Worlds" (Hayley MacGregor and Linda Waldman) 126
Virchow, Rudolf 130
viruses 43, 67, 133; *see also* COVID-19/coronavirus; Ebola; pathogens; West Nile virus
Vogelnest, Larry 36, 37, 40, 95, 96, 99, 108–109, 122, 127, 132–133, 134

Waldau, Paul 123
Waldman, Linda 126
Walzer, Chris 37–40, 77, 78, 93, 107–108, 113, 117, 124, 125, 127–130, 134
West Nile virus 39–41; *see also* zoonotic diseases
What a Fish Knows: The Inner Lives of Our Underwater Cousins (Balcombe) 61
Wilbert, Chris 84–85
Wildlife Conservation Society, New York 77, 99, 107, 117, 124, 127
wildlife veterinarians 2, 37, 43, 129
Wolfe, Cary 100, 117
Woodford, Michael 43
Woods, Abigail 11, 114–115

Zooland: The Institution of Captivity (Irus Braverman) 8, 9, 22
zoometrics 117
zoonotic diseases 1, 2, 39–41, 131, 133, 134, 135; *see also* COVID-19/coronavirus; Ebola; West Nile virus